NOTES ON THE POSSIBILITIES AND

ATTRACTIONS OF EXISTENCE

BOOKS BY ANSELM HOLLO

POETRY

& It Is a Song
Faces & Forms
The Coherences
Haiku
Tumbleweed
Maya
Sensation 27
Some Worlds
Black Book
Notes & Paramecia
Lingering Tangos
Sojourner Microcosms
Heavy Jars
Lunch in Fur
With Ruth in Mind
Finite Continued
No Complaints
Pick Up the House
Outlying Districts
Space Baltic
Near Miss Haiku
Blue Ceiling
High Beam
West Is Left on the Map
Survival Dancing
Corvus
AHOE (1)
AHOE (2)
rue Wilson Monday

ESSAYS

Caws & Causeries: Around Poetry and
    Poets

SELECTED TRANSLATIONS

POETRY

Some Poems by Paul Klee
Red Cats
William Carlos Williams: Paterson
    (in German, with Josephine Clare)
Allen Ginsberg: Kaddisch und andere
    Gedichte (with J.C.)
Gregory Corso: Gasoline und andere
    Gedichte (with J.C.)
Paavo Haavikko: Selected Poems
Pentti Saarikoski: Selected Poems
The Poems of Hipponax
Pentti Saarikoski: Trilogy
Mirkka Rekola: 88 Poems
Kai Nieminen: Serious Poems

PROSE

Jean Genet: Querelle
Franz Innerhofer: Beautiful Days
Olof Lagercrantz: Strindberg
Peter Stephan Jungk: Werfel
Lennart Hagerfors: The Whales in
    Lake Tanganyika
Jaan Kross: The Czar's Madman
Rosa Liksom: One Night Stands
Lars Kleberg: Starfall: A Triptych

PLAYS & SCREENPLAYS

Bertolt Brecht: Jungle of Cities
Georg Büchner: Woyzeck
François Truffaut: Small Change
Louis Malle: Au revoir les enfants

ANSELM HOLLO

Notes on the Possibilities and Attractions of Existence

SELECTED POEMS

1965–2000

COFFEE HOUSE PRESS

MINNEAPOLIS

COFFEE HOUSE PRESS is an independent nonprofit literary publisher supported in part by a grant provided by the Minnesota State Arts Board, through an appropriation by the Minnesota State Legislature, and in part by a grant from the National Endowment for the Arts. Significant support for this project came from the Jerome Foundation. Support has also been provided by Athwin Foundation; the Bush Foundation; Elmer L. & Eleanor J. Andersen Foundation; Honeywell Foundation; James R. Thorpe Foundation; Lila Wallace-Reader's Digest Fund; McKnight Foundation; Patrick and Aimee Butler Family Foundation; The Pentair Foundation; The St. Paul Companies, Inc. Foundation; the law firm of Schwegman, Lundberg, Woessner & Kluth, P.A.; Star Tribune Foundation; the Target Foundation; West Group; and many individual donors. To you and our many readers across the country, we send our thanks for your continuing support.

COFFEE HOUSE PRESS books are available to the trade through our primary distributor, Consortium Book Sales & Distribution, 1045 Westgate Drive, Saint Paul, MN 55114. For personal orders, catalogs, or other information, write to: Coffee House Press, 27 North Fourth Street, Suite 400, Minneapolis, MN 55401.

Good books are brewing at coffeehousepress.org.

LIBRARY OF CONGRESS CIP INFORMATION

Hollo, Anselm.
    Notes on the possibilities and attractions of existence :
selected poems, 1965–2000 / by Anselm Hollo.
        p. cm.
    ISBN 1-56689-115-9 (alk. paper) cloth edition
    ISBN 1-56689-113-2 (alk. paper) paper edition
    I. Title.
PR6015.O415 N68 2001
821'.914--DC21

                                                00-065890

10 9 8 7 6 5 4 3 2 1   FIRST EDITION
PRINTED IN THE UNITED STATES

These poems were originally published, some in earlier versions, in the following books and chapbooks: *& It Is a Song* (Migrant Press, 1965), *Faces & Forms* (Ambit Books, 1966), *The Coherences* (Trigram Press, 1968), *Haiku* (with John Esam and Tom Raworth, Trigram Press, 1968), *Tumbleweed* (Weed/Flower Press, 1968), *Maya* (Cape Goliard/Grossman, 1970), *Sensation 27* (Institute of Further Studies, 1972), *Some Worlds* (Elizabeth Press, 1974), *Black Book* (Jim Garmhausen, 1974), *Motes & Paramecia* (self-published, 1976), *Lingering Tangos* (Tropos Press, 1977), *Heavy Jars* (Toothpaste Press, 1977), *No Complaints* (Toothpaste, 1983), *Pick Up the House* (Coffee House Press, 1986), *Outlying Districts* (Coffee House Press, 1990), *Space Baltic* (Ocean View Books, 1991), *Near Miss Haiku* (Yellow Press, 1991), *Blue Ceiling* (Tansy Press, 1992), *High Beam* (Pyramid Atlantic, 1993), *Corvus* (Coffee House Press, 1995), *AHOE: (And How on Earth)* (Smokeproof Press, 1997), *Hills Like Purple Pachyderms* (Kavyayantra Press, 1997), *AHOE 2: Johnny Cash Writes a Letter to Santa Claus* (Writers Forum, 1998). Some of these poems were previously gathered in *Sojourner Microcosms: New & Selected Poems 1959-1977,* © copyright 1977 and *Finite Continued* © copyright 1980 by Anselm Hollo. Reprinted here by permission of Blue Wind Press. The author wishes to thank everyone involved in the production of these books and also every editor who first published the poems in magazines too numerous to mention.

Contents

DEDICATION

I dedicate this book
to my daughters
Kaarina and Tamsin
and to the memory
of my son
Hannes
(1959-1999)

NOTES ON THE POSSIBILITIES &

ATTRACTIONS OF EXISTENCE

& It Is a Song

1965

Air, to Dream In

Leave it, leave it

    behind the dark
    window the owls
    calling out to each other
    my voice to you
             only heard
  there in the dark
  treetops of the sea

    red the moon rose
    cooled off shrunk
    to a coin in the blue

alone   it is if it is
a poem for you

The Red Piano

      A red piano
he says
      a red piano.
I never saw one.
I knew a man who had a red typewriter,
he hardly ever used it.
      A red piano.
Would it be lighter to carry upstairs
than a black one?
      A red piano, a red piano.
Let us think more musical thoughts.

Faces & Forms

1966

La Noche

the wind   let loose in the dark
and the lights of the city   moving

the city is a great dragon   it is a procession
        it is on the move

but the curtains are drawn
the music unheard

see   men and women   preparing themselves
for the long journey across a room

The Low Black Square

for Josephine Clare

is a table
once upon a time
its legs were longer
but I sawed them off
I sawed and sawed
one of them always shorter
than the other three and so
it got a little too low
in the end

kind visitors breathed
"ah, Japanese"

and on the black square
the tile-red cylinder
in a pitcher we found in Venice
there are flowers
they are flowers

they're just some flowers

The Coherences

1968

Introduction

the poet Vallejo invented new ways of walking
sitting lightly   on wooden Metro benches
not to wear out his trousers
not to wear out his shoes

in the secret code of his poems
he describes those inventions

The Empress Hotel Poems

I
Just get up
and sit down again. Then
   you can watch the dust
      settle.
Or wait for the Irishman to come round
knock on your door again. Twice
   he's asked me
first, the time, and then
"would you know of anyplehs I could get a job sirr —
      lehborin', that is."
They won't take him, he looks too
purgatorial. Poor soul
8 days over from Eire
     where they have strikes.

II
Typewriter banging
better than radio   for company.
Sheets of translation pile up. Too many
   words, too many
other men's words
     bang through my head. Why don't they learn English
in Finland. Why don't they learn Finnish Swedish German
   in England, Old and New.
They're just being kind to you, Anselm.
   They don't learn,
     you earn.

III

The old housekeeper lady downstairs
    likes the stamps. She says could you
let me have them if you're going to throw them away
      anyway. Mr. Burroughs she says
    always did that, he always
      gave me the stamps. He got a lot of
        mail, too.
I give them to her. We are
    Burroughs Hollo Saarikoski Ball
      we are Mrs. Hardy's
    nice writing gentlemen.

IV

White smoke from Battersea Power Station
    rises   moon star London city light
beam from the airport
sweeps the sky. I switch the room light
    on and off and on, light dark light dark.
      It occurs to me
    I'm trying to tell you
      what goes on inside me.
        Out there
      they'll suspect
      a Chinese spy.
Ha. Battersea Beast on its back
pushing vapor puffs through the soles of its feet
      for fun.

V

Go through my things
    god knows what you'll find. When I'm not here.
I'm not here, in this poem
I'm in another room, writing praises
      of their loveliness and terror
the ones that dance through my mind
        not endlessly, but to be one, at one
              with them
          I want to be.
        I want to be one,
      I want her to be one
    when the voice begins
  she is, and she dances.
I am the voice. I praise.
There is
no mind.

VI

To return and find
2 men in gray suits who have come to look at me through their eyes
    and say Mr. H. is this yours? You know they're illegal
      in this country. Oh I didn't know.
    Well they are, you better get rid of it. OK.
They go, and I think
    it is a good thing to have more than one room.
What would they say
if they found what I have
in the other poem.

Instances

I
nice place ya got here
the messenger said
to her whose island
it was
        but the boss
give an order
let the guy sail
back to his own

II
there he sat
by the shore
broken nose
missing teeth
balding
        old dog
thinking of elsewhere   as always
traveling hard   in his head

III
where she was
a moment ago
there is only the wind
whirling up leaves
in her form

long train of leaves
carried by   known to be small
though invisible   hands
while someone is playing a tune on a reed

IV
O Athenaia
fix up the old dog
make him look good to her
again
        eating her famous
celery salads
drinking to her
with new eyes

    flexing
    his toes
    under the table

V
like a trajectory of tons
metal and flesh
hurled down the street
in the living light

his anima
drifting ahead
leading him into it   and through

when he got to the other side
people looked different than he had thought

VI
came up from the cave
patted him   told him
time now
        to go

"who said I wanted to go?"

VII

who walk in back of the back of the real
"beside you"
            the term intersection
a crude imitation of what they are

your known dead are your gods
beautiful but inaccurate
metaphors of themselves

who comes
            has words for it
will be worshiped as men on horses
in Malinche's country

For the Sea-
Sons and Daughters
We All Are

sea   the ships
going out
coming in
passing by.

carry
and hold.
there are lights
in the harbors.

going on
going out,
going
on.

hold
the living,
carry
the dead.

see   the lights
lead us on,
to friends
and loves:

hold on   take care
keep warm
fall
   softly
if and when.

The Coherences

I
for whom the
electric
organ   rolls

girls
          born in the fifties
dance
they have souls
                    and carnation pink petticoats

again
          someone died
he wrote
I could not understand it but thought it beautiful

the animals went in two by two
but the chimera went by herhimself

twelve thousand days and nights
these brains have been lived in

II
now again and now still
moon in the branches
                Luna 3's remote control hands
total recall   total loss of total recall
almost coincident shapes

lid   and   lid

eye   eye

III
a sea   at the end of the street
a burning ship on the sea

the glass door swung
he saw what moved stop
                         then the eyes
the ball
         in the air he already knew
as the ship approached he reversed the glass it receded
the sedan chair's curtains closed with a rustling sound

fingertip thoughts
the flawless   the flaws

a small lifetime
                  leaftime

IV
how to live in this
                     the last age
though there is street
                        and household electricity
I had tried to return from two different places at once
   not knowing I had to be everywhere

"you have such young hands"   and old feet
 it had grown more than halfway down her back
 a sound as out of three hundred
                              Rolling Stones
    as she approached

v
whorls and wakes
drawn through the air
the gestures'
                dotted lines
who can write on them
      unrepeatable figures
can you tell me the way her foot was gently swinging
      perhaps here I could
                                he replied in the dream
the eyes
        swung open
        allowed him to see
shooting star trail graphs
                                rhythms of millennial dances
the variations
                under all music and song
      and even
                soundless
                        speech

Isadora

lines written after seeing Ken Russell's film

I
splintering laughter
the burning man-scorpion raises his eyes
the ladies stand up in a circle
nothing but sky and fast-moving cloud behind them

II
this tribe believes there are those among us who would become angels
later we see them on television and they are ghosts we would have loved
     to have known
had we known what *love* meant, or *angel,* or *ghost,* or *tribe*

Buffalo — Isle of Wight Power Cable

I
writing a letter he said
"this instant in time"
but what was that instant
if not where they were

II
in the neverness motels of the bitter country
lovers lie sleeping and waking in fits and starts

III
empty
        milky sky
above the building-brick town with its captive dogs
baying at night and in the mornings
the radiation
you opened the door and it hit you

an air of metal and transmutations

IV
the cars kept flowing past and into the tower courtyard
but when they stopped no one got out of them
he was waiting for no one
whom did he want to hold
                                    here in the next town
far away too

he had won the race but no one was cheering
slowly he drove up to the starting line

Possible Definitions of 'Beauty' and 'Happiness'

babies
cry

all
different

                         fat
                         woman

                         light
                         shadow

sleep

wake

room

                         cicadas

                         think
                         in
                         sound

                         how you walk through my mind

myth
her name is

soft soft in the dark

The Charge

Small metal box I was given
with a length of black string
            the fuse? no
        it won't light
                no fire
only his ashes of eighty years
into this hole in the ground.

Burial
the law demands
in his cold country

Can't keep your ancestors
        on a shelf nor give them to wind sun and rain
they must be dug under
mummies bones rotting flesh even ashes go
                into the ground.

Hold the string gently
        it slides
across my palm
goes slack: *son*
                bury your father
is the law.

A scholar
he had the face of a chieftain
it haunts me
        the sense of that hole being far too small
to contain what I left there.

Le Jazz Hot

talked to my father again in a dream he seemed happy
perhaps a little older than the last time   told me
he had discovered something called "le jazz hot"
and found it of some interest

The One

           the one
long hair in my beard
           this morning
makes me smile:
                   it's yours

Haiku

1968

5 & 7 & 5

follow that airplane
of course I'm high   this is
an emergency

giant Scots terrier
I thought I saw was known as
Taxicab Mountain

brown photo   legend
"serene enjoyment" they suck
pipes bones crumbled back

night train whistles   stars
over a nation under
mad temporal czars

round lumps of cells grow
up to love porridge   later
become The Supremes

lady I lost my
subway token   we must part
it's faster by air

❦

"but it is *our* world"
tiny blue hands and green arms
your thought in my room

❦

sweet bouzouki sound
another syntax for heads
up to the aether

❦

in you the *in* moon
its rays entwined in my mind's
hair   hangs down right *in*

❦

viewing the dragon
there they ride slim through my dream
Carpaccio's pair

❦

slow bloom inside you
the mnemonics of loving
incessant chatter

❦

far shore Ferris wheel
turning glowing humming   love
in our lit-up heads

switch them to sleep now
the flying foxes swarm out
great   it's flurry time

wind rain you and me
went looking for a new house
o the grass grows loud

FROM

Tumbleweed

1968

Chanson

after Pierre Reverdy

when she wouldn't be there
when he would be gone
from that place and its days
a bird would have to go on
singing
all night

time when the wind
blew across the mountain
white peaks of the mountain
they lay on the sand
hidden by rocks
time, then
nothing else
let a cloud walk by
the cypress trees are a wall
the air full of dust
her hair still damp

when they parted there was still someone
to wait for them and to hear them out
a single friend
under the tree:
the shadow they'd left there
getting very bored now all alone by itself

Tumbleweed

on "the day of great routes"
he remembered a head of tumbleweed

yes once we traveled together

tumbleweed
looks like the skeleton of a brain
if a brain had bones

day and night it travels
the great routes
propelled by the wind

looks startling comical even
the first time you see it
but cannot look where it's going
has no eyes

is dead yet moves at speed
sometimes caught up in barbed wire
or meeting its kind at the foot of a wall
until the wind   turns   drives it on

is like something
in the soul

Maya

1970

Man Animal Clock of Blood

the animal runs
it eats   it sleeps
it dies
          goes the old song
and then
the great cold
the night   the dark

in the dark the man runs
he stumbles he hurts
      his face   the world is hard on his face
he is in love with the world

lord of creation   he wears his shoes large
      make way make way
he does not think of that night
he is warm he will love her if only whenever
          he finds her

if only he could go without eating
if only he could do without sleep
if only he could hold her forever
he need not die
                  goes the old song
                  in his head

and he keeps on walking and wanting
the beautiful goof   walking and
wanting   make way for the lord
idiot   flower   awkward   man

That Old Sauna High

to make the vapor bath
a frame   3 sticks
meet at the top

stretch woolen cloth
take care
the seams are tight

a tent   and into it
a dish
with red-hot stones

then take some hemp seed
and creep in

the seed
onto those stones:
at once
great smoke!
"gives off a vapor
unsurpassed
by any bath
we have in Greece"

410 B.C.
eyes watering
by candlelight
Uncle Herodotus
penned these instructions

adding "the Scythians
enjoy it so
they *howl* with pleasure"

getting so clean
all clean   inside

In the Octagonal Room

to see
Blake's Earth
Mother Christ

    1790
    the color of
    clay

holding small
men to his breasts

to see through
the blood
that flows from

    the inner
    hinge of
    the eyelid

        in '62
        when darkness
        prevails

        cruelty
        blinds you

where
such clarity
rests

Bits of Soft Anxiety

for Philip Whalen

dreamt: crossroads
drove straight ahead
arrived then with some confusion beating of wings sound of great engines etc.
in a strange country where things kept falling on him and out of him
they didn't hurt but caused some anxiety nevertheless
maybe they were just cherry blossoms
maybe it was just his old difficulty of remaining in the upright position of
        the higher primates
maybe it was May
as it was in the other place where he spent most of his happy waking time

Your Friend

he said this
he said that
when pressed
as to which
he said nothing at all

in his country the weather
was mostly rainy

he tried to ride horses
they didn't go   or went
too fast

he punched them in the head
he fell off them

he tried to love women
tried to write poems

even his fellow men
their wives their children and cattle
he tried to love

but he didn't know
how or what was
or was good for him
at all

whatever it was
it kept punching him
in the head to make him
fall off

so he blamed them for it
all of them fellow men women
children cattle poems and horses

many a rainy
day you could hear him
yelling "it's all
your fault"

after that things
were all right for a while
until the next try

Sunset with Blame

you started it all
    and again
        she said   *you*

       THE BLAME
    came rolling straight at him

    chanted
       I'm yours I'm all yours

     into the sunset
    he rode with it

The New Style Western

the two horsemen
on opposite banks of the Rio Grande
shook
their fists
then solemnly turned
their knob-kneed steeds
and rode away

they would be back
but not in this movie
which was about the strange and amusing ways
prairie dog
owl and rattler have
of living together

Elegy

the laundry basket lid is still there
though badly chewed up by the cat
but time has devoured the cat
entirely

They

active mostly at dusk or at night
secretive   living mainly in mind
or underneath stones
in shore zones

Rain

One evening, as we were lounging in his apartment in a relaxed mood, sniffing a little ether, Charles Baudelaire said to me: "You know, everybody has seen rain falling — most people have, at one time or another, actually noticed it."

I agreed, with a chuckle. He continued, "You know, I think we can be fairly confident that it has been raining, on and off, for a very long time!"

Having said this, he collapsed on the chaise-longue, in a veritable paroxysme; but as always, there was a tinge, a definite tinge of bitterness in his merriment.

"It would be absurd to imagine," he said, "that rain could ever have behaved in any way different from that which we observe today . . ."

After a moment's crystalline silence, our conversation drifted to other topics — the day's gossip, the inexhaustible genius of Edgar Poe. But when we stood on the fire escape, taking leave, he gazed over my left shoulder into some indefinable distance or abyss and said, almost dreamily: "It is for ever washing the substance of the land into the sea."

Any News from Alpha Centauri

I

the dog suddenly punched the back of his knee with its snout
short snap of teeth he stopped shouted hey your dog bit me
in the dark street the other man swayed and will go on swaying
thick weed in the sea of remembered nights

                                             an event of no consequence
but for the small marks on his skin in two days they faded
not as persistent as cigarette burns on his hand and arm
the previous summer he'd stayed so drunk he believed himself Orpheus
many a man before him   delusions of a like nature
well dogs never gave *him* no trouble did Cerberus know the good dead
by their smell was he blind as most of them are did cat people ever
enter Hades

               a little of that goes a long way he thought
walking on in the frosty night with the stars as stately
as ever up there any news from Alpha Centauri
they have their own scene there pretty small pretty quiet
a fortnightly newsletter printed on green gas

II

laughing all over her face her body swung
into it too she was telling him something
she was such a joy he didn't know where to look the cat
came in he looked at the cat but it did not enter this moment
how years had changed them   how they had taken his memory
sometimes he thought his mind away
every instant of waking a new start often so slow
he made many mistakes per hour
the cat lay down in front of the fire
and she had already turned into another
lovesong worksong

                   dark soon in the winter
there was hardly any time to stay

awake to think out a sentence like that
one movement
              she gathered all objects in out of the light
where they hung in the room about him
how "years" stood in the air in his place a dumb idol misnamed

III
in the bar there was a photo of Albert Einstein
a photo of Franz Kafka in the rented room

"Louisiana Man" by Bobbie Gentry in the bar
Mozart and The Mothers in the rented room

eyes and voices   screens of solitude
he remembered the touch of a pair of hands

iv
walk in the house of light it said in the Indian legend
walk in the house of light and it walks with you around you
wherever you go

there is only one can give it to you
only she can give it to you
she smiles it stops raining the world will not drown
you walk in the house of light

v
it moves across the big water through many dawns
it goes uphill it stops near the crest of the hill and opens
all its doors

He She Because How

one A.M.
            and she has been sleeping
two hours
                is still asleep

didn't marry him 'only to sleep'
but does now
                sleep

because she's tired because
he's been unkind? because

feeling her bones through her sleep
on the floor in their other room

because she's her kind of woman
because he's his kind of man

and because she is sleeping
                            he's writing
moving a few of his smaller bones

words like love and hurt
kindness unkindness blindness
ecstasy jealousy anger
sweetness
            that too
sweetness of making it with you

how do those words hang together
how does his hand move the pen

how do he (plus) she (equals) it hang together
on their still beautiful

(though in his case
                    slightly bent) frames?

two A.M. questions
now make him sleepy too

he'll go wake her up

they won't feel the same

Traveler

he was of the kingdom whose people bring destruction
love to wound kill and mutilate
                              for diversion and amusement

over them reigned a red personage
always inclined to hurt strike kill

but sometimes seduced by the fair-faced queen
of the other kingdom
                              whose people were charming
loved gaiety and festivities
whose natural disposition inclined them
to the good and the beautiful

when they heard of evil and ugliness
they were seized with disgust

a woman reigned over them
all men believed all women were of that kingdom
unfortunately this was not so

so he decided to emigrate
to a kingdom whose people were tiny and slow
who passionately loved the arts of the writer
the sciences of the stars   theurgy   magic
had a taste for subtle occupations and deep works

we haven't had word from him since
they probably changed him utterly
or dissolved him in aqua fortis

As It Is

there are snippets of understanding
and there are snippets of connections between these snippets

at best   there is a vague memory of details
which have recently been attended to

like reading the Whitehead snippet
recalling a redhead snippet

De Amore

I
love-I   — thou —   me-off-pissest

    Hopi Catullus

II
sponges are simple
colonial animals

attached and submerged
they grow

in autumn some sponges
form gemmules
small round structures

when the colony dies
in cold weather
they drop to the bottom

and the following spring each gemmule
becomes a new sponge

reading this I can see
old love what it was
we forgot

III
consider time
             mon amour
   identities of time
a time of days   a time of fishes

drops of time   each drop
      with its own skin of surface time

and when I'm with
                        and partly within you
      it's a moment of time
      "devoid of any temporal spread"

IV

the Power Return on the new typewriter

strikes the glass

the wine goes all over the desk

I love you

everything's changed for the best

Sensation 27

1972

it is a well-lit afternoon
and the heart with pleasure fills
flowing through town
in warm things

yes what do you know
it's winter again
but the days are well-lit
what's more
they're beginning to stay that way longer

that is a fact
and I am moving
through a town
in a fur hat
the third one in my life
or is it only the second?

the expeditionary force
will have to check up on that
back there in the previous frames

while I move forward
steadily, stealthily
like a feather

I am a father
bearded and warm
and listen to words coming through
the fur hat off a page
in the Finnish language:
"when there's nothing else to do
there's always work to do"

my father said that
in one of his notebooks
and it's true

I walk through a town
and up some steps
and through a door

it closes

now you can't see me anymore

but the lights go on, and you know I'm there
right inside, working out

in love we loaf
munching love's load

it is a fortunate condition

it is a preoccupied porcupine
going about Mother Maya's business
on an ardent spring night

taking this deep a breath is ardent
like diving
up up and away

keeping the harp in tune
even here, where we are

America, no one knows you
but loafing and loving
upon your mighty body
remnant mind and trembling heart
we may yet escape

"Planet X goes kablooey"

"bang bang! wowee! that's neat"

no it ain't, son

except in the most particular way it happens
continually, in your skin
your flesh, your bones, your art

which is what keeps it going, you understand

At This Point, the Moon Starts to Take On a Little Brown and Gray as Opposed to Being so Very Bright as it Appears from Earth

up in the Andes
an old Peruvian
in a featherwork mantle
sits listening to his god

his god is playing looney tunes
on the organ of novelty

while down below in Iowa City
a small Dane is freaking out in a drugstore
shoving and beating on the other customers
yelling this is my drogstore my drogstore
get out get out

the proprietor calls the cops
and they take him out
because it isn't his drugstore

a large unclear device explodes in Alaska
furious hurricanes sweep through the banana fields

old man in featherwork mantle
knows the innate beat of all things
he is engaged in expressing unobservable realities
in terms of observable phenomena

a great body
of tender and intimate works
to sleep beside him
later
like a large friendly lioness
who loves me
the old Peruvian

After Verlaine

after Verlaine
right now
it is raining in Iowa City
but it ain't rainin in my heart
nor on my head
because my head
it wears a big floppy heart, ha ha
it wears a big floppy heart

Dining Out Alone

through two layers of glass
the far end of this restaurant
a man
whose head is
a glob
of light
like anybody's
any body
he is formless form
by means of Maya
and all her daughters, assumes
innumerable forms
of which I am one, dining out alone

Autobiographical Broadcasting Corporation

eight years behind a microphone — blip —

then bid farewell to normal speak

Double Martini

do you remember
I ask the stewardess
how madly in love we were?
when we were four years old

no, she corrects me
not four but fourteen my dear
fourteen through seventeen

and here we are
twenty years later and in a dream

her memory seems unimpaired

I kiss her fraternally
then go for a walk round the plane
in the surrounding blue

and through the window I can still see her smiling
smiling, moving along, serving the lords of this world

Zooming

for Tom Raworth

she looked on him and
the moment she looked
there was no part of her
was not filled with love of him
and he too gazed on her
and the same thought came to him

"Math, Son of Mathonwy"
two thousand years of formal design
romance, or: the goodies
we do get off
on those
as the big bird goes thundering through the sky
way up above the humpback whale and his cante jondo
the rose and the sword in one word is weird
"hey, Miss
may we have another pitcher of gin?"

he placed his hand on her shoulder
and she set off and he along with her
until they came to the door of a large fair chamber
and the maiden opened the chamber
and they came inside and closed the chamber
and no one ever saw them again

but an unceasing flow of wonderful sounds poured forth
from that high radio tower

and there's that word now
walks past my window with two humans inside it
as yet unaware of its horrendous designs

Antioch, Illinois

why are the Bronze Men chasing Hercules?

why does the automobile go GRRAAHHKK! and stop altogether?

because things in the sky go kah-boom

because the water hose burst

Strange Encounter

megalomaniacal
midgets
exist
but
uneasily.

yes,
officer.
no,
officer.

my name is
Kid Sky.

I live in
the elevator.

"you're under arrest."

To Be Born Again

inside my mother
I make a little fist
and then I punch her

enter another plane
walk right into it

the roaring begins

a few hours later
I stride ashore

"welcome to America"

"th-there's a l-lot of b-bastards out there!"
William Carlos Williams

one moment please
to adjust machine

two A.M. in bed
says "come on out"
some one in my head
"you've been forgiven"

the force of being she released in him being
equal to the creation of himself the universe was a place
where he would always want to find her touch
her get lost in the space
ships hailing each other with all their lights on
wires humming and speakers roaring
and a cup of mint tea with honey

cloud of dust or roses (rosé) in the head
of that intelligent monkey face man (Rilke)
high on another world
another time

country and western time
earrings horseshoes clear lethal fountains
laughter shaking his Mother Maya's body and his

as he makes her his mistress
for ever or as close
as you get a book

or drive the big white 'car'
with the black 'interior'
through the exterior and its turning leaves

grew up in Finland
the south of that land

father philosophos and writer
wrote the works of Cervantes in Finnish

mother a talker and talker
all over the known world

but really my parents
you were giant white rabbit people
very wealthy and powerful
lived in a palace place
under Elephant Rock

thrones
robes
and a great golden light
strobed out from behind them

Elephant Rock

the huge weight
and granite shape of it

ten times the size of our house

billionfold growths
over its back and sides

the only country
ever known as the features of god

1939

just sit here telling myself all these stories
when the sun is shining
on the granite and the veins in it and the veins
in the back of my father's hand

pine needles moss and the light the light

a great roaring silence
so spacious and hospitable
to the rising voice of my mind

one of the pines has a bend in it
three feet off the ground

the horse's back
about two feet
the neck then stretching straight up
to the sightless head of it

where it becomes so fine
there's no way of telling what goes on there

where was it I
fell asleep in the afternoon
and down
and into a hall
where forceful as ever in her big chair
he who was I there saw her
hum to a thin corner shadow
the brother pale rigid
not a sound then the sister
energy out of a door on the right

but I knew where he lay
went on and entered
the room light and bare
no curtains no books his head on the pillow

hand moving outward
the gesture "be seated"

I started talking, saw myself from the back
leaned forward, spoke to his face
intent, bushy-browed
eyes straining to see
in to mine

"a question I wanted to ask you"

would never know what it was
but stood there and was
so happy to see him
that twenty-sixth day of April
three months after his death

FROM

Some Worlds

1974

it is said the Chinese believe that the human eye

contains a tiny being of the human shape

which indeed it does, even here in the West

those tiny beings are my dearest readers

Once in Khairouan, south of Tunis, a yellow Kabyl dog bit
me. It was the first time in my life, and I decided that he was
right. He was simply expressing, in his own way, that I was
in the wrong.

Thus Rainer Maria Rilke, in a letter to a friend. This
Rilke was a man who loved dogs and had a profound under-
standing of them. One of the *Sonnets to Orpheus* is not
addressed to Orpheus at all, but to a dog. It deplores the diffi-
culties of communication between men and dogs, and I wish
I could say (now, half a century later) that those problems
have been solved, or that these very words are in fact written
by a dog. But that would be telling a lie, and should a dog
read this at some time in the future, he or she would imme-
diately recognize it as such.

anyone, say, a girl named May
who watches
    say, Humphrey Bogart on the late show
go through customs in Hong Kong
                     may, years later
if she herself actually goes
   through customs in Hong Kong
feel she is reliving the past,
           the past
       customs in Hong Kong

    oh, absolutely

Things to Do in Salzburg

walk, alone
the narrow lane from St. Peter's
to cemetery, and Abbey Tavern
"Doctor Faustus drank here"
come home late
wine-warm, high on air
think of Mozart, Don Giovanni
think, "I could really stand it here
for quite a while"

       in 1926,
       as my father.

Black Book

1974

World World World

for Edward Dorn

the frightened camper watched the apelike monster
big computer is watching you
I am watching a huge
tree-cutting crane
rise up against a Dutch Elm
and cut it down

☞

"algmagtic, keek, de ghroote clomp-cameel!"
I'm truly sorry
man's dominion
has broken nature's
social
union

glassy stare of dying
albatrosses not at all unlike
glassy stare of
men women and children

this was a magnificent specimen of the giraffe

observe its glassy stare

☞

it is known that the Pygmy tribes
in Africa actually live in meadows of marijuana
and smoke it all the time
any chance that could be
what stunts their growth?

probably not
the Watusi tribesmen smoke it all the time, too
and they grow seven feet tall

☞

"at the lake they found an old blind one
who had been left behind
they gave him food
but a straggler coming along later
shot him as he was crawling
to a spring for water
his bones lay on the ground for years
after the country was settled
his skull hung on a bush"

☞

the oysters
brought from Long Island Sound
opened up
at the time the tide would have flooded
Evanston, Illinois
if that town had been on the seashore

the scientists were delighted

the oysters were disappointed

☞

El Presidente grinning through twenty
seconds of TV footage uttering total gibberish

for edifying experiences we must look elsewhere
out the window for instance
we see a great big crabapple tree in full bloom

71

now of course it's just a tree
someone planted it
a number of years ago
probably a greater number than they had to go
many trees
live in the city
some of them right in front of windows

a gentle breeze animates their extremities

❧

we much prefer
the noble face
delighted
with its nobility
to the stupid face
delighted with its stupidity

❧

for a fistful of dollars
however small
one is this transplant
heart over fist

"dead skunk in the middle of the road"
in the radio, not on, but in
total privacy, but with a number
of little robots plugged in

❧

as Giorgio Piccardi the astrochemist once remarked
to be subjected to cosmic effects
one does not have to be shot
into space, one does not even have to leave one's room

one is always surrounded by the universe
since the universe is everywhere
as remarks are not literature
and this is a poem:

wear the head as it grows
keep the lights blinking

through her whose name is desire and cherish
all bodies, that they may fit
their faces
that they may fit their bodies

⌒

automobile at indeterminate speed into sunset
and in its giant
Council Bluffs rays
the goddess
and all her ladies-in-waiting
                              waiting

⌒

Chairman
Mao
Ursula
Andress
on the bingity
bangity
bus

⌒

A. Wallace Rimington
inventor of the lightshow
continues with us
a beam in the system

73

antlered with desire
in the cryonic pools
between dream and day

we rule all of the heart
the great heart
and the does

walk by
and the nights sing
in the sunne

the sunne
a good mama
a very loud star

Märchen (Beginner's Luck)

one day
Ted Berrigan
got kissed
by a toad

he instantly turned
into a tall
beautiful girl!

the toad
in its turn
became Ted Berrigan

it was the first time they tried it

No Money

the last Empress of China
took all the money
and turned it into a giant marble steamboat
that's why there is no money

Classroom

seas of tranquility they sort of nod
when you look at them as if to say
in a little while it won't exist
not even on postcards

Tremendous Wind and Rain

tremendous wind and rain
whipping down the avenue

on the corner
the plate glass breaks
and the blonde in the ice-blue evening gown
comes tumbling down
into the running man's arms

just as his hat
flies off and is
run over
by our trembling automobile

in New York City
home, for many years
of the poet Paul Blackburn

now a resident of Paradise

The Walden Variations

for Robert Creeley

white hair
fine fringes
under the brim

old sunshine on twigs

grandpa
a sturdy
alchemist

old sunshine on twigs

❧

old sunshine on twigs

and on the pigs
we ate
together
he and I

deaf alchemist
loud grandson

❧

ate together

teeth fell out

and died

old sun

Indian Summers

on the wall
vine leaves
in his eye

the warmth of their color

nature
he thought
nature
did I miss out on nature?
all these years

two pigeons were walking
across a green roof
above the vine leaves
which were red

they were too much
like people

he wished they would go away

when he looked up
they were gone

and there is talking
and no end to talking

no end to the things made out of human talk

Motes & Paramecia

1976

Song 1

big ball of ivy
green and serious
a chimbley
in the sky

at dusk they spin round it
the high-pitched brothers and sisters

nor is the cop
in the helicop
ter above them lacking

in either the sensuous or
the metaphysical dimension

Song 7

in a garden of flexors and extensors
in a cool room to work in

"with peaceful tool"
where the quality of

affection is affection
the soul grows arms to hug itself

in the middle
irregular columns of leisurely horsemen

Hector Sir Launcelot Lemminkäinen
Quanah Parker

move down the main spoke, or
is it up, into the light

most speak of as maybe the sun
flanked by the laughing

jeux d'eau
it is good to see them so

happy at last, the music a
slow malagueña

good to see them go
the beautiful, deluded uncles

Bicentennial

we weren't here
a hundred years ago
nor will we be
a hundred hence:
and the fireworks were just average.

Life 2

desire

in the home:

the greatest

Message

Hello!
I am one of your molecules!

I started out from Crab Nebula,
but I move about.
I've moved about for millions of years.

I entered your body, perhaps as a factor
in some edible vegetable,
or else I passed into your lungs
as part of the air.

Now what intrigues me is this:
at what point, as I entered
the mouth, or was absorbed by
the skin, was I part of the body?

And at what exact moment
(later on) do I cease to be
part of the body
i.e., you?

Let me know what you think.

Yours,

the beetle wakes up.

it is unconscious.

that is all right.

La Cucaracha

the new members of the orchestra have arrived onstage
to replace the old ones flung into the pit
after a brief tune-up the concert will resume

FROM

Lingering Tangos

1977

You

three times as many of you
as when I was born

Info

for Joe Cardarelli

a bunch of gods
struggling acrost the swamp
bent under rain's weight

what kind of info is that
where did you get it

I didn't know it was info

sure it's info hell you know it's info

here comes another contingent
these have hovercraft swampshoes
and geodesic umbrellas

hey wow that's some good info

nightfall image:
lovers, supping
in the concrete pueblos

their windows
lion's eye yellow

lives upon lives, contained
oh, one wishes, graciously

in the greedy o greedy so greedy
land? suppose it still is, a *land*

we can only stay tuned or stunned

Saturday

we sea monsters
came out of the sea
now we be land monsters
trying to become space monsters

Heavy Jars

1977

awkward spring
has spilled its
golden ink
all over the angels' bibs

and off
the swan's soft chest
white feathers fall
into the swamp

and so forth

and I thought I was

a big and perfectly sensible dog

with some dignity

thinking not of form number 0412 dash 70144

but of a city

equal to my desire

Helsinki, 1940

exploding, shattering, burning

big lights in the sky

and this was
heaven's gate?

no no it's just the front door
same old front door you know from the daytime
and we're just waiting for a lull in the action
to cross the yard, get down to the shelter
and meet the folks, all the other folks
from all the other apartments

and there was a young woman
at least ten years older
he thought very beautiful

blankets, and wooden beams, and crackling radios and chatter

it was better than heaven, it was
being safe in the earth, surrounded by many

all of whom really felt like living

slowly
the eye scans the page

the heart
beats steadily

while the mind winces in
in infinitesimal
spasms of
almost pre-natal pleasure

down in the street
it is divided
into three parts:

sidewalk, street proper,
sidewalk, large things
of equally inelastic matter
on either side

these, inhabited
by homegrown beings

several of whom are reading too

the karmic revelations
of so many
silly and lovable cells

conjoined in the bliss that feeds
them, and on them, too

thus holding them

(now turn the page)

In a Tin Can Mirror

"she was a love child
  he, a premeditated one

"theirs was a splendid house
  color and form and sound
  munificently swirling
  whirling and twining
  within and around, above and below
  the flora and fauna of their lives"

well said, but not
what I wanted to say

the music is playing
the dog is sleeping
I am thinking
of one gone upstairs
and why I'm not there

because I am a stupid old fuckup, that's why

and there's this herd of cows
keeps mooing fiercely in my head

and that's a lie
and you know it

moo, moo, moo

"the hind end of a cow
  not at all that attractive to us
  is bliss to her boyfriends"

same old jungle
same old machete

certainly, always, talking

summer nights
when I won't sleep
I sit and beep
these signals
out to you

oh, I don't want you to weep
just want you to
keep me on!
this sounds like a song

by some miserable creep
but that is only
partially true:
the other part

is really very manly,
independent, capable
and so on

maybe. bullshit. the demands
are entirely self-imposed
and senseless, if met
round anyone else's corner, that
objective place —

yes, they would be that
there, all right.

summer nights
or winter nights
or spring nights
or autumn nights

the wars of the heart

sure as hell aren't righteous

the language
comes loose in the head

the lights in the driveway
signal my neighbors' coming and going

it always is 2 A.M.,
as I am

and yet, in the woods there are marvelous places
my daughters go there, every day
bringing home armfuls of mint
and their own fragrant faces

to counter the general grayness and sense of mala suerte
graven on those worn by the males in this tribe

who persist in confronting, confronting
horns lowered
facing the emptiness to be populated with foes

Hannes, I love you.
you are my son.
we are the boys.
we are the men.
we do learn to live with the fact
of the language, thus confronting us
with division, which is the nature of all

that moves, is born,
and leads a life,
and gives it on.

it is the thinking
no doubt, it is the 'thinking of'
those forms:
the gigantic
breasts, buttocks
equal to them, and yet
the absolute
necessity of *face* —

with, perhaps, a rose?
in her mouth
and arms
upthrown, in the sign —
the sign:
hands joined, or touching

a circle, above and around the head

("hail Isis!
"you don't say?")

"oo-ee, she gives such good head"

Professor Wilhelm Reich
makes one feel like a squiggle
(squiggle)

hello. how do you do. and the folks
all around you, still
'stock-still'
trees in the clearing

and that is the only
time you'll know it is there,

still hanging there, still
in the air
between our bellies and faces:
yet it is
always there

dear, dear.   dear
Stevie Smith, poet

and fellow woman,
where is
the cloud
of energy you were

the gentle wit and in-sight, equal
in every respect
to the most perfect body statistics
I ever respected

no way you are dead

you were such a good head

Big Dog

I bring you
this head,
full of breath-
takingly beautiful
images of yourself

and put it in
your lap.

Now I breathe
more quietly.

Now you pat me.

Now I sigh.

In a moment or two
I'll get up and
be a man again.

Dedication: A Toke for Li Po

born in pa-hsi province
of szechwan
lived muchos años
at the court of the emperor

ming huang, but was banished
as a result of falling
in disfavor? with the empress
kao li-shih, & wandered about china thereafter

only occasionally attached to a patron
leading a "dissolute" life, addicted? to drink
writing the poems about the joys of that life

notably wine, & woman, & all the rest
& agitation of the sensational universe

came to his death by falling
out of a boat & drowning
in an attempt to have intimate intercourse
with the moon
in the water

one of those of
whom it is said:

"he took the charge well"

Lunch in Fur

1978

memory   rain   pride   wind

she's not here now to say
your hair looks lovely

tears soak his head
he cannot sleep

night deepens   he taps to the FM tunes
driving the sky car of the recalcitrant self
through other lives   there is smell of burning

leaning by incense   he sits till dawn
having talked all day   and then kept silent

stuffed white devil
stuffy Chinese

John Coltrane
had a love supreme

note tacked onto surface says
bring the form

bring the form   to the crazy weaving

kicking Manhattan to pieces every night
her face softened as she saw the visitor
utter a shrill mocking laugh and crumble
the cactus roared and the powdery substance
timely and shapely   blew away

remember the fun we had ramming
the fresh cigars between the teeth
before the infernal biochemical clock
covered us with its rampaging goo

maybe we better get back to the office
the world's largest cluster of oversize lungs

the mind travels wildly among its planes
think of the fun I missed when I was sealed up
I'll get even for that   I'd rather loaf than work
but I have to eat   especially at my age
the only way I can work is to practice astrology
since that's all I know how to do   but at night
you should see this kid at night

the frail silver-haired woman darted across the black lawn
dashed into the cottage then quickly tipped
a bottle of the red medicine to her blue lips

Po Chü-yi heard them   Lawrence warned us against them
the chattering parrots in the painted halls of Orc

heart embittered by understanding
sisters   brothers   stranded in strange lands

flesh and blood   cast adrift on the road
as we watch the bright moon   there should be tears

there will be a day when the dust starts flying
even at the bottom of the sea

animation subsides into terminal slapstick
it is a como se dice cathartic
flying kick in the rump-shaped ego
which then immediately changes
outward aspect to weeping brain

the Cathari believed in something they called
but knew wouldn't necessarily come when called
were right about that
while insane on who we are with our bodies

"they started it all! they started it all!"
and yes we burned them (salut, brother Blackburn)
had our revenge   now have our consequences

how many goddamn words for the one
they thought they had

in the Marshall Minnesota Quickstop
burger joint   I encounter objects
on objects   glass on table   purse on chair
refracted light on more refracted light

how obsessive   this universe
how bone-aching lonely to boot
(bones aching inside of boot)

then it starts coming back   the way
you say the word "whole"
and "yes I like it"
cher maître of Odin House

how it is both the hole we fall into
and the one we come out of
the one we should visit with understanding
how it all rocks and rolls right through the pain
making the light come through

forty-three years   such wonderful
if also horrifying times
and they stay with you   crowd up around you

if not always affectionate   always insistent
they'll never leave you

With Ruth in Mind

1979

Or, to Hocus the Animals of the Pursuers by Changing Their Dream Cassettes (Old Thibetan Trick)

for Tom Raworth

cold and windy   cloud with delicate
cottonwool monkey face   drifting by
frittering   violins   on the radio
tape   drifting by   the magnetic heads

and into the spaces   between other heads
magnetic   electric
from here to everywhere
possibly back   and on out

what is it like what is it like
some   recall a   musical theme
by having the score's image
appear before them   then reading it

it is conceivable that what we call
remembering   in a human being
consists in her seeing herself
(mind's eye)   looking up things   in a book

thus what she reads in that book
is what she remembers
Wittgenstein Zettel (scrap)   six fifty-three
estuche inglés el papél márca bambú

"is the baby out yet"   "no not yet"
when they listen to it   it must dimly remind them
cats to Mozart   tape drifting   zettel drifting
someone blown clean down the block

shrieking with merriment shock

105

time travel back again   hopelessly stranger
tremulous listener
heart embedded in cliffside
sea lions bark at it   hungry and curious

many friends quite crazy
plant on table trembling
many-talk-in-head   my name

the bats are hibernating so now
the birds   hunt   the twilight
later gigantic   motorized   beetles
scour   the night

Poe Dog   requiescat   morning glory
blooms but an hour
cause and affect   dynamic
we have no sure means of knowing

duration between   each death and birth
the seeds of karma   dynamite
little paws folded   big paws folded
stagecoach takes corner   plenty of dust

the idiot wars of the young
the idiot wars of the old
master babe mandragora
shrieks when torn out

shrieks when rammed back
needs warmth inbetween
appearing   reappearing
uttering language in extracurricular states

goth space   general restlessness
wolfed down bread and meat
among the boulders in the huge scarred seam
a dwarfish person of the queen's retinue

adorned on the upper side with a strongly accented
border of interneural spots
he said nothing but waited
playing with the hilt of his dagger

they usually keep a considerable distance above ground
he thought   above the surface of things
as one who had never seen a mirror might wonder
in what depths of it lay the face she saw

hillsides open meadows disused quarries
seaside cliffs narrow valleys
running down to the sea open downs cornfields
roadsides borders of woods even the woods themselves

apelike he silently disappeared
into the darkness   we are pleased to announce
he had three concubines   famous for their beauty
apelike he disappeared silently into the darkness

this is a fine bright form she thought for my clansmen
live far apart both on the upper and under sides

we'll find a way she whispered never fear but kiss me
notwithstanding the abruptness of this introduction
set like a stone he took a deep breath
paler shades and two oblique lines

rather less oblique than usual
in one swift rush all was clear to him
it had the appearance of being sunk some way beneath
north toward the high mountain village

there is a hill track branching off
her hair streamed out like the wings of a raven
of a uniform deep green almost shining
he began to flee from her

but ever she followed him chuckling
sitting on flowers in the hot sun
moving the hind wings wheel-like in evident enjoyment
at the first light of morning

pairing usually takes place in the morning
from neck to ankles she was covered by her head
holding itself upright on a tall culm of grass
the people came out staring and pointing

their whispers rising like surf all about her

☙

the wind kept hitting the house and shimmering
in the moonlight he approached
it was impossible to guess in what respect
the form approached obscurity since the description

flatly contradicted every peculiarity of the latter concept
large instead of small and weirdly bright blue
her features blurred and swayed before him
throughout the room there were broad grins

like fire in dry grass
the larva winced and contracted
directly an ant's foot touched it
a bead would appear and at once be imbibed

his words welled up like stones in the pool of faces
and since she saw no tangible manifestation
of his presence nor any attribute of him
she found it hard to concentrate and slowly closed

antennae waving over and upon him
dawn and the braying of horns

☞

melancholia   early developments in physical existence
cause us to experience certain attacks of paralysis
one had only to turn over the stones to see this
and then get into the chariot   with quick   uneven steps

thinking   gloomy and wild is the air of this place

☞

heat waves raced and shimmered round the basin's rim
in limpid space suffused with sunny beams
and then the axe was loud   so fine it was to be crazy
mused the archon   look   the mutant metaphors

take wing
wiping the milk off their whiskers

☞

having meditated much on airy things
unimaginable distances and cosmic pie
I think I know what the white poodle dog thinks
perched in his window across the street

he doesn't   I like him
he's both eminent and reasonable

eldritch cries of the wind among turret tops
stared at the dark faint outline of hills to the east
intoxicated in the glimmering starlight
lying back upon a low couch

spring you get for free she thought and mostly it doesn't
turn out too well but then life's strength lies embedded
in a fresh coarse evenness
dense like any good production of Mnemosyne

on her knee the flare pistol lodged securely in its holster
a prime star shell in the breach
permanent event in the stream of change
followed by another and another

yet slowness and sun have stayed with me
in calm and gentle absurdity she thought
slowly the ice of the unformed universe dissolves
saw the dark blot against the white stair waver

move down to merge with shadows   "why are you here"
afraid it might be the ultimate horror
foretold in legend   "completely normal person"
but it was just a máquina working by springs

moving talking laughing on its way to the shop
toward morning we begin to feel insubstantial
our knees cease to shake we wrap ourselves in our cloaks
and walk to the grove of oaks
twisted and windblown   clutching the stony planet
with roots of authority   purple and scarlet

frequent narrative climaxes   moments
of great suspense   and moments out to lunch
may be saved by one's ability to characterize
one's mythic role   by comic ineptitude

the slow Finn in the houses of those-who-cannot-speak
not the swift one   gliding through hermetic glens
from dawn to dusk he sat in his chair   gazing out
at the ghostless panorama of disintegrating cones

Zapotec killers stare   stone-eyed and deified
there must be a way out of this shirt
P.G. Wodehouse probes the drift of cloud
the thing says this   o bless all humble

the thing also says   that's not a shirt
trees and language   in and out of the hat
sure-footed he flows from tussock to tussock
uttering cries of revenge

mighty breathing   sacred rapture   frantic screams
sounds good   thanks   tremulous frenzy   thanks
concealed behind a canopy of palms
whence issue strains of delicate music

from an invisible angklung   she leans
across the table toward her companion
unfurls herself double time as fighting breaks out
among the maniacal jitterbugs

retract periscope
I will return   for my change   another evening

III

who sold you that machine gun a warlock a mind
open to total disaster   enlightened
facts and figures mere ghosts
occasionally encountered as described

this is the song of Irgud   we're living in Zomboid
where drowsiness lays its thick fingers upon us
even while we are trying to get the money
to be ready to hand it on when it is our turn

he looked about at the faces of his counselors
intent and it seemed to him full of accusation
he began to speak in a sharper tone   a quaver
clenched pale shaking fingers in snowy beard

mysterious indeed were the ways
there were invisible cities   rites of the goddess
outside and above   or were there
well there are tangible and intangible gifts

but not on a silver platter
the worm starts under similar pressure
meeting in vortex of tattered posters quietly flapping
back and back   before it goes forward

incorrigible intimist   mon âme
to hocus the animals of pursuers by changing
their dream cassettes   old Thibetan trick
Joseph Cornell knew it well

Finite Continued

1980

Behaviorally

it is possible to state
the case for pigeons
as sensibly-behaving
organisms

and against poets
as schizophrenic
humanoids

poets
emit verbal responses
i.e. write verses
that produce
few pellets of food

and even fewer
food surrogates
such as money or fame

thus B.F. Skinner has said
without meaning offense   he said
that poets are not
sensible

Southwest Minnesota

here our antennae bent
                          but did not break
here we were told
                    "you talk broken
and once you talk broken
                              I guess you always do"
here our friends flabbergasted our students
"they just didn't seem like your average
language instructors
                        the way they didn't
seem to care about sentence
                                  structure
punctuation
              or grammer
that doesn't mean
                    I didn't like them
though I thought these artists were interesting
I was confused
                    I didn't know how
they could publish
                      some of the things
they did
          who would buy them?"
still there were ways it was muy bueno también
not at all like TV
                      but truly philobatic
here comes a letter saying "please tell me
what does it mean
                      this word 'philobatic'?
I have looked in all major dictionaries
with no success"
                      well my dear Major
success is not it
                    but "go in love" does it

115

The Years

i.m. Charles Bukowski

I met her at the West End Bar. I mounted.
I felt disgust and horror. I did feel some
pride. I left town. I came back. I had
some beer. I saw it. I opened the bottle
of wine. I saw it. I began to notice.
I could feel the tears. I sat there and
drank my wine. I was fairly drunk. I did
feel some pride. I could barely see. I
was a dog. I lied. I left town. I was
not a very nice fellow. I had some beer.
I came back. I walked toward the truck.
I saw it. I didn't feel it. I got up.
I began to notice. I could look out at
the people. I took my bottle. I looked.
I could barely see. I felt disgust and
horror. I opened the bottle of wine. I
had some beer. I met her at the West End
Bar. I mounted. I broke her false teeth.
I was a dog. I saw it. I began to notice.
I left town. I climbed into bed. I sat
there and drank my wine. I didn't feel it.
I was a nice guy.

TV (1)

"for he is Ishi   the last of his tribe"

"couldn't help noticing your aftershave"

the brain which takes that in its stride

is yours and mine   and it is late

TV (2)

funny
Nazis!

twenty-five years
pass.

then,
more funny Nazis!

No Complaints

1983

Manifest Destiny

to arrive in front of large video screen,
in pleasantly air-conditioned home with big duck pond in back,
some nice soft drinks by elbow, some good american snacks as well,
at least four hundred grand in the bank, and that's for checking,
an undisclosed amount in investments, and a copacetic evening
watching the latest military techné
wipe out poverty everywhere in the world
in its most obvious form, the poor

Songs of the Sentence Cubes

"badfoot:"   "candy:"

white   big
 wife,   baby
  walk   girls
   fast   kiss
    leg!   small
this   old
 man   boys
  old;
   bad
    foot.

                  ⌒

why,
    we
      hear
          some
             fly
               ate
                  your
                     new
                        work?

it
  got
     your
         old
            lady,
               you
                  dirty
                     beast.

*

later,
        man.
it
    one
        cold
            time.

*

had let what kiss taste face
                        clean forgot

time took it out
                & how
                        but slow

Doc Holliday

The silences grow taller
the other end of the line

Sporadic punctuation
of human exclamation

"Katie?"
"Doc?"
"You there?"
"You going?"
"You gone?"

Cards, shuffling through
faint honky-tonk

☙

Saddle up
at least once more
and ride like hell

in pursuit of unattainable
sanity, joy,
"calme, luxe et volupté"

just hoping the storm
won't rise, blow you under

not too far down at least
for the tribe

to dig up bones, doings, sayings
of the once happy beast

The Images of Day Recede

the pleasure principle tends to start squeaking after a while

just like this wood frame canvas chair of mine

does to remind me that nothing related to human

activity is simply automatic, or predictably continuous

Romance

"suddenly in a light shawl
you slipped out of the half-darkened hall —
we disturbed no one,
we did not wake the sleeping servants . . ."
　　　　— *Osip Mandelstam, translated by David McDuff*

suddenly
    in a bright shawl
you slipped
        in the pitch-dark hall
waking up all the servants
         & twisting your ankle
but I picked you up &
        flung you into my rickshaw
      galloping off
    as all the lights
        came on
          in your former home

☙

you swept down the hall in a ravishing gown
& I, I swept you up in my arms
& together we rolled down the stairs, & the footmen
gathered us up and deposited us in the taxicab
& it took us home, to Nubar Gulbenkian's place
where we had been staying these past eighteen months.

☙

you stumbled, & fell. the pint of vodka slipped
out of your hand and bounced down the chute, alerting
the guards. we looked at each other,

held heads, & kissed:
there was no tomorrow, but *they* were fucked, too —
the pint contained killer gas. the label
read "no one gets out of here alive."

☞

I came shinning down the vine to you.
your pear-shaped breasts quivered at my descent.
Once in your arms, I found myself in the jet
serenely zooming across the Gobi Desert

☞

you stood in the driveway, smiling
& I apologized for not having been there

you said oh no, I was looking at your house
& talking to the animals and all the plants

around your house. & now we are here
& we can go in.

& we went in.

Dirge

comes a time you know every move:

"change the musicians whenever you like"

comes a time "it's all over
                    by the time it hits K.C."

comes a time someone called Erik Satie
& someone called John Lennon
"look-alikes"
are equally dead

comes a time some you gets shot through the lungs
four times to collapse in historic Dakota hallway

(someone called Panna Grady no longer lives there)

comes a time you travel all the way from Honolulu
in fellow incarnation
possibly "Chapman"

comes a time you don't know nothing

and all the musicians are gone

you missed it: they didn't miss you

                              8 December 80

Ten Cheremiss (Mari) Songs

walked
        in the woods: a green leaf
brushed
         against my face

it wasn't a leaf:
           I had just thought of my lover

☞

come, let the two of us
go pull up some leeks!
we'll be together,
one soul around us.

☞

a white blanket
             onto the back of a white horse
a silver saddle
         on top of the blanket
a down pillow
          on the saddle
a wax candle
         on the pillow

you can make a wax candle
longer or shorter.

you can't do that
with your life.

at dawn, a dark cloud appeared
firing lightning bolts at my father's house.
why do I keep telling my dreams:
who but me understands them?

woke up early,
went and carved my name
in the bark of an apple tree.
contemplated what I have
and what I don't have.

in the dark before dawn
we walk through the woods,
talk, whistle, and sing.
don't listen to those sounds
as if they were songs.
they are the sounds of our pain.

I shouldn't have started these red wool mittens.
they're done now,
but my life is over.

climbed the hill,
went down into the valley,
followed the whitewater stream.
if the dream comes at all, it comes at night,
to allow us to walk in our thoughts, in the hours of daylight.

⌒

snow coming down,

                  rain coming down,

there's room for it all

                      between sky and ground.

and the troubles we have,

they all fit

between heart and liver.

⌒

you dream you're traveling through water.

thus, you emerge from grief.

No Complaints

for Robert Grenier

HIGH PLAINS DRIFTING

on the high plains
when we meet
the inspector
we say "buenas tardes, inspectór"

꩜

ON THE PHONE

"when do you go to bed?"
she asked me.

"when do you go to Tibet?"
was what I heard.

"never," was my reply. "I've never
felt like going there."

꩜

good
        to do the little
physical
            things
in the lonely place
sung by
        the ancients
                            we swim to meet

＊

too little and too late

too brittle and too fated

we are but rabbits that pass at dusk

＊

parenthesis

the part in her hair had a little bend
                              at the end

Pick Up the House

1986

Valid

Having a pasaporte, how much more *valid*
I am than brother Jesús or Pedro
trying to swim the river,
tackle the razor wire!

Some

Some thing falls
to some floor.

Someone remembers,
makes much of it.

The other one says,
I had no idea.

after the telephone
he sat a while trembling
the way dogs do when nervous
when they've perceived something
much larger than their brain

Sorpresa

cool
      April wind
blowing
         mulberry
petals, belated
             "snowflakes"
in the small
merciful
hours:

came
      home,
walked into bathroom:

aahh! colors!
pretty shapes!

your
      summer clothes
shedding their wrinkles
and mothball scent —

doing
      the things
I've been trying to do
ever since you told me

come in   come home

Page

In measured hand
we write the letter
full of rage

but then
a little later
feel our age

and say, shit —
who's that do?
Some bodies

gun their cars
out of this street.
The sun

also rises. Nancy
and Sluggo
go to it.

On the Occasion of a Poet's Death

The dedication and intensity of the dead
always were greater than ours.
No doubt it seemed that way to them too
as dusk was falling
on their last weary glimpse of a land
populated by twerps.

The disembodied glories of Hades await us.

Letter

Dear sister, where was it, where is it now
we sat under a tree, and you were crying, and
I did not have the faintest as to why . . .
But I did. I knew it was because you were in love
with Col. Hercules Wilmot Scott, and there was no way
that anyone was going to understand *that*.

See You Later

Ascending mountain path
in good company: Ted Berrigan
seen here the first time after his death —
Duncan McNaughton, still alive in the world I'm adream in,
    many others
wearing sturdy United Beloved Nations overcoats, blue-black,
scarves, gloves, goodly shoes
though there is one fellow with snazzy hat:
turned-up collar prevents me from seeing face
— Tinker Greene perhaps?
                          Well anyway, here we go
in bright blue day,
mountain to our right,
sheer drop to miles-away valleys
on our left — the path
beautifully paved, with pale gray almost square chunks of stone
the width of it
a person and a half

so we tread lightly and with care
while typically smoking this or that
(doing this in waking life
we'd be gasping, stumbling, quite easily gone)

Ted says, "Wouldn't you know it?"
apropos of what? There's also a strong wind
and I am worrying about the emerald abyss
to my left
           yet confident we'll all make it
to wherever we're going that seemed
just around the corner
and now is, quite possibly, not merely

atop a mountain
              but *inside* the mountain,

only to be reached
by an equal number of strides
                                 down: on the inside: no shortcuts.

Hair, beards, coats, scarves flapping
in the emphatic wind
glasses reflecting pale brightness,
we're walking, bullshitting along, just as in
real life. Hey, here's George Kimball III
with a bottle: thanks, man: who or what "won?"

But careful now, one slip and we won't
feel so great anymore. On we go
Ted our guide, friend, beloved raconteur . . .

Aeons later, someone, Duncan I think, says "You know
we're going to give it back to them"
and I think oh no, what's this? We're not just proceeding
to the most remote tavern of the universe?

And Ted says "Yes, yes — we're going to
where the pounding of acceptance
meets the pummeling of negation — no, no"
drags on Chesterfield King
"which is utter benighted bullshit, of course"

Now there is sleet, even small hail in the wind
and I remember the waking lifetime we strode
through blizzards in Minnesota, early Iowa morning rain
and youthful demons on Lower East Side

and I think, there has to be a trick, to end this dream
the way there are tricks to end a poem

Put in a Quaver, Here and There

It is smooth, fairly uniformly gray, and of a topological con-
formation not easily described by Euclid: circa two inches
wide, one inch tall, and half an inch in thickness. (I am
indulging in little twinges of nostalgia, using those ancient
premetric and soon-to-be-forgotten measurements.)

It is a rock found on a beach called Half Moon Bay, an easy
hour's drive south of San Francisco, picked out from among
a great number of fellow rocks and pebbles, ground and
washed ashore by the Pacific, the most intimidating and also
most beautiful body of water on this planet. The reason this
ocean artifact now sits on my desk, facing St. Paul Street in
Baltimore, is its sculptural aspect. It has eyes, nostrils, and a
mouth, all in unexpected places, making it what the French
call *une jolie laide* — a beautiful ugly one, easily seen as the
fossil skull of a small Venusian, landed long ago on one of
Earth's shores. A miniature Henry Moore, it defies easy
recognition, arrests the eye, and makes one think of other
possible forms.

While knowing well that it's just a large pebble, pointed out
and handed to me by a friend with whom I'd spent hours and
days on that beach, watching dogs chase pelicans' shadows
across the shallows, I also know that it is what the ancients
knew as an "object of virtue" — irresistible — recently trav-
eled to visit its shore of origin in another friend's purse, as a
mascot. It did indeed bring her home safe and sound.

Daniel Spoerri, Swiss artist-philosopher, friend and disciple
of the great Duchamp, made a book called *An Annotated
Topography of Chance*. This consists of a detailed description
of each and every object found on or around his studio table
on a given date, complete with the history of these objects'
origins and relationships to present circumstance. Looking

139

at my Venusian from Half Moon Bay, now serving as a humble paperweight, I am reminded of Spoerri's fabulous undertaking, and — what with a post-thunderstorm July sun shining into my window — encouraged to suggest to all of you, dear friends, moments of contemplation vis-à-vis accumulated objects of virtue in your immediate vicinity: Mute witnesses, they could yet prove to be guides.

Late Night Dream Movies

to Christopher Toll

I
The war beneath the seas
is quiet.
St. Paul Street, Baltimore, at 1:30 A.M.
is not.
But I'd sure as hell rather be here
than in some sinister submarine.
I don't know — why
am I telling you this? Who are you?
Yelling out there. Well, I'm yelling
in here too.

II
Heavyset self-assured fellow
at marbletop café table
keeps pointing at peacoat
suspended from Martini Rossi parasol
and saying "You mean you don't *have*
another coat?"
Shivering
in my underwear, I rage back:
"That's the only coat I have!"
Grab his lapels, haul off, and,
almost connecting
with his hateful Sidney Greenstreet smirk,
wake up to Jane's startled yet smiling face
and her saying "You just punched me in the chest?"

III
Now we are in scenic Iowa City
in a motel

with sliding glass doors fronting on Olympic-size
patio swimming pool: it must be some kind of
conference — here comes Jane, with hardly
any clothes on, followed by patently upset and
expostulating Father — she stops, turns, leans forward
and tells him "Why don't you just go suck on a
big fat cigar?" Crash, boom, Rachmaninoff. Next thing
I know we're sitting at table among dinner debris,
Jane at far end, in some animation,
Dave Beaudouin, looking most proper, on my left,
Father across from us: we're having coffee,
brandy, it is quite warm
but Papa has been weeping — his shoulders, even, are wet —
and after sympathetic murmurs and a short pause
he pulls out a musket-shaped clarinet
which turns out to be a cigar holder — affixes
big cigar to it, starts puffing — I say
"But can you play it, too?" He says "Sure" and gives us
a tune. I think this is quite certainly better
than last night's number, when I was climbing
the scaffolding of a giant roller coaster
in order to get back to my life, my words.

IV
The castle, cut off by the tide: we're moving in on it
in these nifty inflatable two-person assault rafts, just
before dawn. Granular silver surrounds us. We're
on time, we'll be there right on time. The Great Electric
Eel is our impartial observer: we'll avoid bloodshed. We
owe it to him. Jane smiles at me through the spray: she is
the most beautiful human I've ever seen.
I squeeze her long fingers: "It'll be all right."
In our wake, light-bearing particles dance.

142

v
In our dreams
we cry out. Even if
it is merely the computer
brain sorting
recent days' info,
we do cry out, in our dreams:
some things
want to be heard, attended to,
hugged or killed,
known, before termination. Amen.
"Amen?" Yes,
that's an honest word.

An Autobiography

"Go there!"   "Stay here!"
                "Stay there!"   "Come here!"
What changes
                is nothing but anywhere
they want you,
                and you want them to want you
there: and then
                there you are. Were.
Formerly there,
                now here. What do you know.
What a way to live. To have lived.
Nowhere. "One, very small,
                                to go."

De Amor y Otras Cosas

Sunday: Mission bells at six in the morning
over thousands of small heavens and hells,
well, mostly purgatories. Give us a big kiss.

☙

She changes. She does
what you did not expect her to do.
She'll always do that. It is
her way.

☙

In places
there's a face
in place.

☙

Things
burn
off:

see
what's
left.

☙

Sound of the summer's last cricket
haunting, that night, but all thoughts
of oblivion
banished
by your smile

145

as you moved close, and held, and whirred and pirouetted
your way into my soul, that rarely seen cousin
who lives in the house of memory

⤟

I love
your back. I don't
have anywhere
to go back to
except for
your
back.

⤟

Sweet of you to say
"Well, it'll give you a chance
to spend some time at your house"
while knowing, as you must
that any house I'm in where you are not
quite soon seems empty
until you walk in the door

⤟

The faces
we make making love
are the only ones
will change our faces
over the years
into the ones we deserve

⤟

Insect-clock seasons pass, but the great pleasure
humans provide one another when so minded
is as close to perennial as creation gets

☞

The dances of dusk are slow, because the dancers are.
Yet the dancers perceive them as fast,
excruciatingly fast,
and valiantly marshal their strength and cunning.

Outlying Districts

1990

Diary

One day's
big event was when

the cardboard
box I had set on

top of logs burning
in the grate toppled out

of the fireplace in a lively
state of combustion

Pocatello, Idaho

thin man whacking

away at tire with mattock

in 7–11 parking lot

9 P.M.

Saturday night

we
saw
that
sight

Anti-Lullaby

Wake up from a dream
of a large herd (very verbal)
of porcine politicos

assembled for imminent charge off cliff

Well, that's . . . that's almost interesting

The sun also has risen
and we better get on with it

"early in de mawnin' an de road is gettin' light"

So let's tango on down
    the shining path
to breakfast
    at the Café Spartacus

The Ass Waggeth His Ears

Seems like some of these
younger ones grew up
still believing that old
hype about this being
"a *fast* world"

    the world ain't fast

it's big and sluggish and doesn't
give a shit about your microbial jerking around

    widescreen night stars

    smudge planes slow

    astronomical corkscrew aesthetics

as chemically complicated as poetry equals curved speech

The Tenth of May (1988)

Jane is out being a delegate
    when she comes home
we'll light the candle and have some spinach spaghetti
with Mr. Paul Newman his sauce
his good cause sauce and smiling face on the label

I do add a dash of Worcestershire
    a little garlic and some white pepper

oh Eros we thank thee for thy gifts
this day the day
    of the great book burnings in Deutschland
      fifty-five years ago

In the Land of Art

the artists
work on the art farm.

They store the art they make
in the art barn.

Once in a while, they take some out
and take it to the art store.

When the art store sells some,
they take their share
and put it in the art bank.

Then they take their art checkbooks
and go to the art inn
to have a good time.

Or take each other to an art movie
or an art dance.

They wash their clothes at the art laundromat
unless they are successful and rich and have
their own art washer and dryer
in their art basement.

When the artists take a trip
(an art trip)
they stay at the art hotel.

When they get sick, they go to the art hospital.
And when they die, they're buried
in the art cemetery.

And that's the life of the artists
in the land of art.

Tarp

for Kit Robinson

Warm and soft
or cold and hard

the taco of existence
lies in front of the bard

who remembers
here in the dark

the barf on your shoes
shaped like a backwards question mark

and as you blink off
the snow keeps falling

over The Searchers
and their dim expectations

In the "Hip" Little Bookshop

catering to the local
writing workshop's needs and tastes
(works by the faculty
and their friends)

predictable stylish "fiction"
predictable stylish "poems"

I mutter to myself "but this is
just shit, it looks like books
but it's just shit"

I feel embarrassed
but I don't wake up

it isn't just a bad dream

but out in the street
in the front yards
there are these hyacinths
and daffodils

goddamn little crowd pleasers

"It Was All About . . ."

poor communications

mistaken identity

voyages   battles   sieges and potions

returns

black sails

and dying

in love

after a busy life

Or, What I Remember of *Tristan and Isolde*

In the Library of Poets' Recordings

the dead speakers
we can hear
but the dead listeners
can not be retrieved

Letter to Uncle O.

for Andrei Codrescu

Dear Publius Ovidius
    "The Nose"
missing ah missing the rose
    of Rome
for ten years of letters in verse

in one of them, startled to find yourself
    calling drear Tomis "home"
— a shanty town by the frozen Black Sea
    where people grow fur and look daggers

and no speak-a-da Latin
    but something called Getic
Getic! or at best broken Greek
    and winter is a year long

while you pen song upon song
    to send
where you once were young
    listing your poet friends by name
and even some whose names you can't recall

praising that lovely sodality
    of once-upon-a-time
a welcome break for your reader
    who's 2,000 years too late

to do a thing about the ostensible reason
    for your lengthy *Tristia* or *Drearies:*
the Emperor's pardon

because that emperor lives
    only within the rose
        of a city more perennial

where dream and memory converse
    carouse and conjure
        breathlessly deathless

(and who could pardon himself that way
    except now and again
        between the lines

Idyll

water
the yard o
wild domestic

The Missing Page

It was a poem, the jittery sort

"about" struggling through rush hour
traffic in downtown Baltimore

then, seeing you

there, on the far side of the river

of steel and plastic and sentient bags of water

cloaked and hatted   smiling

perhaps in disbelief at seeing me pass
the second time, in midstream, unable
to pull ashore to let you embark

(it also had some quote from a Godard
— just clumsy artifice)

The thing, the thing was

"how do you say?" immense

          yearning and delight

Alla Petrarca

Downtown
Madison, Wisconsin at night
is pretty quiet. Returning

from the dinner for scholars of Finnish
in black plastic boots that seem to be shrinking
I listen to their heels on the sidewalk and feel like

a German Romantic
a hundred and fifty years younger, enveloped
in my sense of missing you, oh fairest of ladies!

back home in Boulder,
Colorado. It is storybook time, as when we saw
that gown in the window in Stockholm's Old Town

yesterday? Or the day before?
We who are of this gender, what can we do —
we know it must be a burden to you

to appear in our visions as the summum bonum
the great female sun our souls do yearn for
but at least you don't have to do it in person

every time. My feet hurt but I am so glad

(receding footsteps)

No Detachment

step out   snow and sunshine
walking   feels good
two blocks   bank machine
working!   good
on to local market
salad stuff   good
head back   small detour
bookshop   browse   my books still there
good   or bad   not sold   buy
last Sunday's *New York Times Book Review*
more Joyce Carol Oates   oh well
all right   stop   red light
plastic shopping bag on left wrist
shake wrist a little   make sure
watch still on   back home
tuna snack shared with cats   good
sudden good god! realization
watch is gone

retrace steps   look everywhere
house   street   call bookshop
wretched day   watch gone
nice watch gone   rage   confusion   dry
tears   mutter mutter   what's the use
snow   sunshine   life is shit
Roman numerals   lovely
picked out with Jane Dalrymple
me protesting excessive elegance   expense
growl sigh yes
                    an evil iguana tongue
flashed out of the Void today

La Vida

for Janey, "mi vida"

Through swirls and eddies of footfalls
converging, diverging

some soft, some percussive
she walks to work

thinks of the two
happy young people

glimpsed in the car behind her
and how they *glowed*

among thousands streaming along in their shells
under big plumes of dark smoke under heaven

later says "If I wrote poems
those are things I would write about"

and I say, well, that — that's a *movie* —
but later think, no

it isn't, it's *life*
It's life, all right

Brother (D.H.) Lawrence

and all the eerie
'previous' states of mind

in which one was rushing
around inside

of a roughly
spherical tangle of self-
generated messages

and turned up high, for sure,
to the point of despair

ah, the *drama* of it all!

which was exactly what Brother
Lawrence had warned one against

but better reception
came only much later

such as the one
one is enjoying

this radio morning —
his birthday: a hundred and three —

with Ellen Burstyn, an actress
reading his number on The Turtle

Glenwood Springs

Under Doc Holliday's
weary eyes

    last scanned
just before Checkout Time
in that fake Vienna hotel

my lady, rising
            out of steam
(but not at all
"out of steam"

straight, lovely
       as mountains

Arcana Gardens

I
the cat's apprehensive inside her head
'things' are really hopping   a cat

with wings   now that would be a thing
there's this lady now writes her verses

with built-in lacunae   there still remain 'things'
and things to delete

contained in the changing light
moving the frame & things

from room to room I miss you
when you're gone all day

yet when you're home there's times I'm lost again
inside the side
                        shows of my head

in this picture we see an oligarch
flying in his recliner

II
the practice of poetry:
doing it when called upon

oh blast this doglike devotion to the US of A
get ready for MacCommunism

the light inside the body
at the end of long flexible tube

I'm so bit-ter . . .
I'm so pret-ty . . .

    go on up
    or off

bluejay on woodpile
first prize: dinner in Des Moines

second prize: two dinners in Des Moines
well I'm heading for the bedding

the old legacy was a bottle of no anxiety
& one of no grief   those made you high for a while

then laid you low
weird white sugar architecture of that church in Buffalo

the blackness of Gothenburg   permanent diaspora
the ideal state

when the mind / body committee decides
a habit has become immoderate   it's a good idea
    to let it go

III
had to invent religion   ideas of karma afterworld etc.
in order to enjoy ever more highly

structured existence? (requires 'security' 'stability'
less general random viciousness)

an epic of prayers   poetry what you read
when you exercise the *skill* of reading

when tired of record of operatic soprano
(on radio) stuck on the two little words *da capo*

the world is bigger than your head   or even mine

IV
oh it's just like magazines used to be — with poems
by Ted in them

(who wants them to *like* their poetry
as long as they *read* it)

well it's time to be drizzling on
truckloads of stuff to keep us within the framework

but writers of small language groups
their admirable stubbornness

clings to the 'absoluteness'
of their particular language

their words   by extension that's of course true
of everybody

(don't know if I'll ever feel like writing 'about' the times
in life I was a total idiot asshole?)

"I want a longer attention span"
"He wants a longer dick?"

Finns: some general sense of shaggy folks tough
eking out a precarious   up there up Norf

"my metaphor machine is bigger than yours"
all greed relative?   love work that sails close
    to its own parody

169

stand up a berserker   end up a beseecher
in the vast stone forest of the world's war memorials

the ghosts of generals stumble about
disheveled confused   graffiti on the great moving wall

moving toward The Wall   résumés for god
Papa wanted me to marry the Finnish language

Mama   chemistry   (her father's life)
both kept me away from Finnophone women with all their might

so I went to Germania and married a German speaker
but couldn't make a living in those lands

so ended up in London   thus changing
my great love affair with the English (specifically American)

language into a lifetime commitment / marriage

v
old staples-through-the-side books   they *work*
people pay more attention to the righthand page

each text gets equal weight   maybe the species
(homo sap) doesn't spend enough time

looking at admiring coveting what it eats anymore
thought while watching cat watching birds

at feeder on other side of glass   "he had trouble
announcing a formal presence"   gazing at red orange and green

in slowly steaming pan it occurs to me not at all suddenly
that one I grieve for may well be content

to be living completely alone in a universe
of the greatest possible distances

Bertolucci's *The Last Emperor*
a life just like everybody's

the emperor child   the live-forever young man
the long haul to the end

VI
"killed by orthodox reality" (Peter Handke)
a Linnéan classification of poets?

rereading Corso: *that* tradition   the sixties out of the fifties
so sturdy   later poetry much more nervous

viz. Grenier's frontispiece for *Phantom Anthems*
Nerve Man   yet in him as in Berrigan

still that cheek
      & glint

when it degenerates into homily exhortation
or some disguise of those (story / antistory with moral)

it loses the power to drive us happily crazy for a minute
or two totally out
      of our gourds for one of those

         eternal moments
      of *le merveilleux*

VII

cut to Pearl Street in Boulder where frisky yuppies
& even aging hippies go shopping for earrings
we just have this little bit of the haul to do
the forms formalities with which we 'stave off' death &
  thought of it

the common customary ones & then the 'deeper' ones
such as some music some poems

walking in the wild word woods first reading Corso
say or EP for that matter that old strut

that old fiddling while Rome burns canto strut

VIII

weird inverted Puritan desire to prove one's mettle
through suffering stoically and wittily

behind the idea of giving readings
drunk stoned on speed mushrooms acid

(handed down by that Welshman possibly further back)
like the embarrassed drunk father

only when drunk is he able
to admit non-utilitarian emotion

and LDS part of that mind-boggling Anglo appropriation
of chosen people ism

via King James Bible also still active in Aryan
Nations types who claim that Anglos

& "Northern Europeans"
are the true descendants of Israel

172

but the true inhabitants of these deserts and mountains
be lizard and coyote   Paiute and Ute and Shoshoni
    (Bear River Massacre)
present-day natives displaying their wounds
(kid in front of Rio Grande station) & scars

you go out there then you come back in
where the well-meant sentiment meets the hopeful cliché

Hemingway   a bounder & proud of it
the beauty of a genuinely *playful* life

possible?
isn't it?

IX
composing from notebooks   a mobile with sideshows
"and here we see"   here I see cryptic entry Actual Filth
        "Is that *actual* filth?"

some poems seem most effortful   as if their author
had labored   over them

ten hours a day seven days a week   and that's
what's wrong with them   "naphthalene"

mothballs of my childhood   naphtha = crude oil
right (check) trudge trudge (glasses in other room)

o be *glad!* you have
many rooms to walk

instead of having to write all your poems in another life
at Mutant State University   "your own medicine"

173

my mother used to say
"just you wait until *you*" etc.

really just a young 23-year-old American poet (came here in '66)
or should we start in '51   London   '38 in that case

> and here we see
> the analytical
> bent

x
Orff's *Carmina Burana* quite terrific but also quite like
a bunch of young Nazis roaring

well I can't do everything at once
bet you could if you tried

yelling at each other in front of the computer
the sublime just fell asleep and died

but the utter & certainly wonderful *craziness*
of 'analytical language' (Situationist texts

Derrida Heidegger before them for sure) such gorgeous
kudzu lingo   dog noise pollution

"I hope you're not *confusing* the computer"
was it an hour ago I sat there in London wondering

about Ted Berrigan   this tough young American poet
& critic in the pages of *Kulchur* magazine

"the testament of beauty" & what was that all about
well I'm sure it had its share of dog noise pollution

a little vulgar eloquence   yes lowercase american
is what I am   a big invisible fish   on a "chops gig

like playing for eight hours a day at Disneyland"
so little has been written about X

because X's work cannot be paraphrased   this
is the goal of all poetry   it is indeed

impossible to ascertain what X is really writing about or rather
it is that X rarely writes about

but is a manifestation
on the page
                    in the air

XI
Dance of Dada   Dance of Death
it only writes itself little by little

a walk through the desert of many faces
by the fountain of six patina'ed frogs

the houseboy was told off for sweeping *around*
the outside doormats   in the city of New *Orleens*

let's only be classified when dead
& then perhaps resumed   in Spanish dark

& if a little myth comes with the territory
that's always nice   & cleanly temporal

human rights day? the day no government's able
to raise an army

for quite some time the way was to fall in love
& you can put quotes around all of the above

over & over
    hi ho hi ho

child's (my) vision of work as somehow
martially? pleasurable

being "a poet" gives one permission to be a crank & even
a crank in print

but you my species
you're trying to overwhelm the planet
  by numbers?

XII
hooked on English I make six cents a word
no epiphany sans community

the dick came striding down the hall
"goddamn fucking Greek deities again"

old Mozart . . . young Cassandra . . . owls
swoop through the canyon at night

aah am I supposed to say aah? is this
the "aah experience"?

who you asking? dunno
is Robt. Bly around?

we pay the state to kill all those we'd rather not think about
but "a real house with stairs & everything"

you deserve it dear daughter
far more than all the bigdick religious entrepreneurs

who've stuck together
across the centuries

Sam's Bar and Mosque
(a hypothetical place)

XIII
living like happy savages with no TV   Arcana Gardens
& he's fifty-five   my goodness   let's dangle on
    down the street

poetry bookshelves   dear elephant graveyard
Science and Democracy

"even just *thinking* about it
ups your production of benign neuropeptides"

all the words this critter can say
when awed by all the world   up there

Cygnus XI HDE 22 68 68
Black Jewel of the Northern Cross   down here

DIAMONDS GUNS TV's in the Pavlovian pawnshop
string 'em out

them colored lights
then turn 'em off again

XIV
up on into what's this all about
this critter makes up its own rules

177

at the speed
of greed

last night my love got up out of bed and banged
her head on the doorjamb

this evening there's a report on UFO sightings
in Guatemala and it's been very
      windy
            all day

XV
ah Babylon I exalt thee above thy detractors
Babylon is The Old Days   The Babylon All Stars

jazz in the ruins
before the ruins

"hey man I just walked out in my slippers"
when I say I wrote that   it is my intention to state

that someone using this same body did write that
then   yes here we see him

his brain   made that metaphor
mid rock and fern adream   with Chingachgook and Cody

but that man in Angola
said to have killed two priests for criticizing his poems

      boy
            that man must write
      some Satanic verses

XVI
Colonel Walden at Pulkovo   lauded by Trotsky
in John Reed's *Ten Days that Shook the World*

heard on tape on the way to Taos
"HEY THAT'S MY GRAND-UNCLE"

don't burn that flag
boil it & eat it with hot sauce

because I had spent 35 minutes in the bookstore
I felt I had to pay $6.50 for this magazine

I didn't really need then walked off
in the rain past more people resting

dying or dead on the sidewalk
Die Welt frisst was der Fall ist

(the world eats what falls down)
give the homeless $45,000 per capita

and make them *sole* subject of *all* U.S. news for a year
and let every township in the U.S.

have a simulated four-year oil boom
in alphabetical order

with acid trips among
    the gnomes

XVII
on the sidewalk a large
dog turd shaped like the male
    procreative organ

"none shall be permitted to retain their shape"
well sir you may be right   Roxie Powell of Baltimore

calls in the early A.M. he's working on a novel
whose heroes are Appearance & Reality

more power to him he did insist we go find you my love
down in the bookbinder's Hades (climate controlled)

for the rest of the story   see page

XVIII
see page   & then see page
page after page
as it goes along

until "one day" it stops
with a squeal or a pop   but for now let's go on

to sing the praises of a brown-eyed girl
"I met in a country town"
                & love
as light & filigreed but also mud-heavy
    as the old songs

with our glasses slightly askew on our noses

    "time for your Van Morrison sir"

Space Baltic

1991

End of the Range

weep ye protein herders weep
on dead willow hang the mushroom hat
there's no more natives to slaughter
and the foreigners are fighting back

Irritable Aliens

Texas, Texas Jack Omohundro —
your famous cowboy president —
where he buried?
take us there, pronto

Two Parts

I
Listen to me,
Señorita:

when your heart
caws like a crow
groans
like a god on the dole

remember
to remember Poetry
the secret language
the one no parents ever know

II
No kidding
didn't know people wrote like that anymore

where did you get that?

The Place of the Great Sacred Secret Obscenities

you don't say

Yeah   it's like this great bunch of perennial hooligans
puking long streams of it

Angel Wings

High
on the Great
Plan

the believers
glow
in their pods . . .

Well,
"it's all
a web
of words"

the master
(actually,
Bob
Creeley)

said
in a dream
I saw

in Salt
Lake City,
Utah

Home on the Shelf

Yet another
Collected Poems by a friend

In the end
will we all just stand there
doing The Megalith or / and
"We Shall Be Changed"

as foretold by bass-baritones
in Handel's *Messiah*

Oh yes yes yes
changed
into billions of unrelated particles

some perhaps frying
in the grease of the kind
of Chinese-American restaurant
where your best bet is the "chicken-fried steak"

some flying
better than that, in the bones of a hummingbird

Space Baltic

Far, far
        in the future I see

an ancient gringo baron

showing his little grand-nephew
some dusty glass case memorabilia

in the more than half-ruined manor:

"... yesh ... yesh ... we used to call that a *foot*-ball ..."

Cloud Watch

Dear friends   gone into the dot of the giant
      question mark   what to tell you   that the sun
        shines upon the just and the wicked
     as it did when you had some time here   question mark

that the soul still gets the gulps and shivers
      at the sight of grace
    and that such grace still exists
in the street   at the dentist's   in bed   three dots

    that the oligarchs drool
      and twitch "uncontrollably"
   at the sight of god I mean gold   exclamation point
while most of the populace goes on slaving and whoring
        for grub and shelter

      that your musics
        amigos
      still play in our hearts

Answering

An assignment given by Chris Toll of "Open 24 Hours":
"poem with the words: quark, quasars, vacuum cleaner, Mu,
Buddha, and Chevrolet."

the Buddha
is in
in the vacuum cleaner

he has his little quarks

and sure they knew
about quasars in Mu

there may be some
in that Chevrolet

now remember one thing
the task of the poet

is not to comfort
but to give comfort
to the Enemy

Enjoy

enjoy your termites and bourbon

Near Miss Haiku

1991

The Older Artist

Kid's written a 200-page lament
over lost love: now what to tell him?

All the tears in China
won't bring her back.

Time
chips our mugs.

Dive-bombing hairbrush
scores bull's-eye in toilet.

It's a tough world.

Guilty Your Honor guilty
of much haphazardous waste

and too many shoes.

After Ungaretti

i.m. Darrell Gray

the coin
fell through
the beggar's
palm

they called him
Allah Jehovah

they were never quite the same again, tu sais

it got them
right in the video

Paradiso Terrestre

small lemon yellow butterfly

      & Mr. Sidney Bechet

playing the tunes

    of a more confident time

and what sits here

     observing these

is poet

  or hawk

a flying suitcase

    full of mice or dice

Les Américains

"No better 'n cockroaches" — bus driver 5 A.M.
    between Frisco and Grand Junction
referring to drug dealers users and ho-mo-sexuals
    including victims of AIDS

☞

Grand Junction bus depot: square-faced Native American
sits next to Mexican vaquero type
conversing
with elfin tall Black man
    chiffon rag round his head
        holding young fast-asleep daughter

can't hear what soft-spoken Black man is saying
but the rocky Native American is barking
    "Yeah, that's STUPID!
        that's really STUPID!"

vaquero smiles steady no comprendo smile

old refined White lady
    is telling Vietnamese man
        about her childhood in Butte Montana

☞

    Straight, No Chaser

Near Miss Haiku

order out of chaos equals frogs

➥

"here come the faster
       'n a rattler poets"

  o for the day
    we hear that cry

➥

the competition
       for World's Most Virtuous Nation
  has been called off
(offer no longer valid)

➥

Modern Jazz Quartet
    after all these years —
  a bit like when the man smiles
& says "well done"

➥

Max Bruch
      violin piece
  full of glowing
inwardness
      made him wipe a tear
  for his parents and think
(well)
    "one hopes they had their moments"

~

"he probably was a horrible guy"
        "nooo, he wasn't"
     "ok he probably wasn't a horrible guy"

~

"You can say things *again.*"

    "You sure can."

~

                    she had this in-
                    credible
                    urge
                    to tell
                    the
                    whole
                    story
                    all
                    the
                    time

~

early moments of mother
        must've been something!
     she could never live up to them later

~

having picked it out of
        an enormous pile of bodies
     the reader
        opens the book

FROM

Corvus

1995

Born Today

for Jane

is to be one to the one
closest to you
who shares the air
& other elements
right there   next to you

two bodies wrapped in darkness
among millions of other bodies
wrapped in darkness & smoke
war bloodshed & chaos
     voices rising out of the dirt

one to the one   without whom one
wouldn't be one
       who saves one when lost
in regions of the past
raging at bygone constellations
          pursued by a swarm of angst gnats
     who saves one by her sight & sound & touch
to notice
          that gravity's strong on this planet
notice
       there's a half-ton of apples in that tree
notice   cricket jumping on cedar branch
     feline humor   magpie elegance

in sum
       this world
born not so long ago
with maybe not that far to go
       still roaming
     the contradictory corridors

of a universe or two
wind turns pages   then shuts book
he looks up   she looks up from piano keys

        hold that frame

Swing High Swing Woe

sleep
        unperturbed
"no
self"
moment
of blind spot
reached
at last
(margaritas . . . payday . . .)
then up
with a start
in love's arms
to Terra's hard rain
her drums of dread

yet even at zero
once glorious with friends

green light
            on a lizard that caught you watching

let mute edge of night knot a rat

wick wither

            gaze roll out to the dark

like trembling bats

                their petals still coiffed

A Town Dedicated to the Pursuit of Fitness & Inner Peace

says the headline   so that's where we are
that's why they're building
fifty new houses
right next door

now the telephone wants to tell me about a deal
on cleaning our carpets & upholstered things

I tell it "we don't have any"
then replace it quite gently
in what I believe is called its cradle

yes among those alive today
we're truly fortunate
to be living these charmingly specialized lives
in "a town
dedicated to the pursuit of fitness & inner peace"
unlike the majority of the planet's towns
which remain dedicated
to plain old pursuit of food
& staying alive   a few moments longer

yes fortunate   if a bit haunted by Kafka's Fear
of waking up in less delightful state

but that comes & goes
just like the battles of light & darkness

old hats bursting out of their secret closets
to be stuffed back in   to reappear thirty years later
empty as ever (no brains) but plenty of clout

very fit for his age
the Senator
enjoys
his inner peace

Blue March '91

brute metal glee
momently done careening about that Gulf

wind blows dustballs and spiders
out of the walls

> *to sort*
> *black socks*
> *in the dark*
> *is your task*

the Species invented Time
  and probably Space

its function to be their recorder
  until the End

> *young beauty*
> *picks up spider*
> *re-locates it*
> *in flowerpot*

Note Found on Meditator

war bonnets horsemen a waving forest of lances

      a lovely sight

     if you don't care for what they're attacking

it's John Wayne they're attacking OK no problem

      beauty

knows no ideologically correct routines

      beauty knows nothing at all

that's why she asks all these questions

Inhabited Eyes

falcon-eyed Montcorbier
gone complicated after much dying

sang about April
in nimble remembering

calligrapher Berrigan
carved the Iowa rain

In the Raging Balance

i.m. Jack Clarke

Energy, the man said, equals
Eternal Delight. Does our return to it
mean shedding all that was our art?
Task of The Living: to ask questions
of The Dead. You did it well, you
Weird and Funny Dude! I thank you
and wish you a good Eternal Night
in Tunisia or wherever you've taken
The Show. "The winds on the moon
blow so cold, so cold" could be a refrain
but isn't nor will this last line rhyme
with anything but tears then again why
should it be the last line and come to
think of it it couldn't possibly be

Why There Is a *Cat Curfew* in Our House

Wake up 5 A.M. to this *yattering* in the kitchen
think: they must've come in through the cat door
switch on light see three teenage raccoons
at the cat food   but now confused
trying to walk through walls complaining louder
not heeding my hoarse "shoo — shoo"

Uh-oh! cat door *flies* open! & with a growl and a snarl
in charges 35 pounds of furious Big Mama Raccoon!
explodes into house   goes straight for bare legs —

startled I slip on the rug fall down the beast keeps on coming
she's getting *larger* I swear she's *inflating* with rage
her young regain courage fan out in attack formation
& do some snarling & growling as well

It is time for reinforcements!
I shout for Jane   she appears in the hall
groggy   stark naked   "what's the matter"
enough to distract this Kali of Procyons

now aware offspring are in good shape
claws scrabbling on floor   she turns
leads fast retreat back into the night

big sighs all around   "hand me the iodine . . ."
so now
we lock the cat door at night
so now you know why
there is a *cat curfew* in our house

& if I were a Victorian poet   there'd be a moral
but late in my century all I can say
is that she did of course remind me of my mother

206

Blue Ceiling

I
raccoon sees Cat go in and out Small Door

    the mental beanie rotor turns

the mammal ever-blissful when it eats

        "ah, Earthlings — "

one might of course say there haven't been any further poets
since Pierre Reverdy

sentence understood only if read at right tempo, said Ludwig

then he wrote it down
and now we're reading it:
      "avoid" "arguments" "with" "the" "furniture"

the magus is dead long live the magus
        semper bogus
(by now we should all know what people really like)

then tried to wipe a smudge of light off the table
with all the fussiness of an old, er, void
    it's all a struggle
cuttin' time
        so mighty fine
you won't be able to verify any of this

II
life's just a dream remember
    poetry just an interruption
of the great conversation

207

farewell notes from those gone
weave through the composition

a father walks in an old apartment
talks: "never admit you're rich or asleep"

as you enter the recording studio
you notice you don't have anything to record

skepsis is contemplation

may you be forever strange
may neither spring nor ashes faze your dailiness

what's ragged should be left ragged

"we want the guided tour!"
slow thoughts down
notice tone and sensation

bus bounces into pothole
with delicacy and precision

III
when you met him he was a man
now he is a postage stamp

you can't open the window this is Dallas

"they took my billiard table!"
Mary Queen of Scots complained in 1576

mice fall from the sky

mind suffers body suffers language suffers
thinking urge greater than any other
bugs in throat in the dead of night

but what's past is yours in the vectors of joy

       in a café named after Beatles song
    person plays home-made instrument
combining tuba violin and gong

the unconsciouses
    slow as hazardous waste
roll through the night

IV
Americans still know how
    they know how
to manufacture a good working handkerchief

    "It's real surreal!" said little Laura

fantasies magicks
    all come from the child
        to work its will on the giants
then it grows up to be a giant itself and then
    there is still
the whole goddamn universe

    "It's never enough, is it?"

the poet you hardly knew
    looks dear and old like you
not like you but old like you
    and dear to you
on the cover of his "Kings"
not like thin dark peacoated figure
    glimpsed from a cab this spring
        strode past Brompton Oratory
    large take-out coffee in hand
his double from half a lifetime ago

v
and the closetful of magical toys
        shrank
    to old shoebox of objects broken and shoddy
now having neither
    you have both

slowly they walk across the sunny parking lot

they
        are your friends

" . . . mad as Cassandra
who was as sane as the lot of them"
        in the footsteps of Jesus Tom and Jerry
perfect their running-in-air trick
    proceed
                at speed
off edge of cliff
perform their mid-air miracles
then plummet back-pedal hover and soar
over America
not to answer the question she asks

        but to return
        the question
        to her
        to change it
        and return it
        to her who asks
        shall be the whole of the teaching

VI
green rhubarb leaf-dragon
dormant under snow
beneath red studio wall

"merely a matter of belief"
in December
or *any* time and (whaddayaknow)
so is the snow
the red the green

the wall the house the art
what keeps it all
from flying apart
if not the love that moves
the sun and other stars

    and around midnight
    raccoon lady
        stops
    just short of the doorway, peeks in —

    trundles back out
        tells her companion:

"No good, he's still there
in his chair
reading Harper's"

Pterodactyls

I

"Publication date first of October"

from Zlatko's Serbo-Croat   via fast translatese French
into "my" English   his journal scrolled up Macintosh screen
these summer months   hoping he lives to see it
I think of him often   & of his city's Utopia of convivencia

"while you are not safe I am not safe"   Ginsberg in "Howl"
when Sarajevo falls   all of us multiethnic bastards
who pray in all the temples   like all kinds of food
& minds & bodies every color shape & size

we better start digging our foxholes in the fourth dimension
& while we dig let us chant We Piss on the Serb Nation State
We Piss on the Croat Nation State   we piss and shit
on all your godforsaken states

murderous money-making machines for greedy sleazeballs
lording it over slaves who failed to teach their masters

II

tread the fine line between farce and pathos
torque your thoughts in the mental (not metal) bookshelf
hermeto-(not herpeto)-linguistic
shrine to Mr. Hun Tun
professionally known as "The Gourd of Chaos"
walk up & down   walk off & on   sleep off & on
far off   far off in the Gobi Desert   what can you say
you can say   & you won't be far off
"I have my love to keep me warm."   & I can say
"'Yes,' he said. 'Yes, of course.'"

then you can sleep it off   & it may well be
what all these pronouns are saying
is merely the tremulous gibberish of just another other
talking to the page with an old child's fingers

III

i.m. Ernest Hemingway

trying to impress felines
strange hairless ape with mad eyes
too tired to explore postmodernism
"a rare   *luckier* kind of guy"
checks in at Perfect Cloud Hotel in Laphroaig
it is 9:15 A.M.   a Fundador brandy, please
yes, he would like to join the Lotophagoi
(old Ez   he wrote it down)
so let's just *decant* it in here
time to wind up the world no more substantial
than a good tune   *oh fairer than the evening air*
marked by slender delight   what we feel
is what we believe we feel   see say and be loved
despite much dull material to-be-forgiven

IV

for Tomaž Šalamun

a long sentence: "son, write longer lines"
a green Pegasus, dancers, yaks
sing, masters of the universal pibroch
sing, balalaika, in the teeth of adversity

but don't you think it's time for Comrade Blank
to retire, with the understanding: *no more poems!*
sing, you "few buckets of water tied up
in a complicated sort of figleaf" (EP)

213

great solar, you stir, wake each exile man
marmoset, mormon, clits and toes
& tiger faces in the fire, Colonel North
got to the shredder in time to deconstruct history a bit

dig, with man, up feeling
here, with Doctor Who, in Deseret

Pounces

i.m. Zoaire, 1974–1994

I
one night loud hissing fills the air
it is the venerable Mr. Zoaire
her gato negro lover & familiar
of eighty seasons

fierce flat & frozen to the ground
outside her studio door
he's facing down a band of five raccoons
fanned out & ready to surround & pounce

she saves him from a warrior's death
& now we lock the cat door every night

but we couldn't lock it against the grim reaper

II
small corner of the weave
he slumbered in the sun

III
So, in the great beyond   I raise my paw
to strike the lyre   sing a praise
of Her who was my life's delight
as I was Hers

    (all that   much more
     in single fading farewell *ping*

& oh, he now says, can't you go on like that?
I really liked the sound of those first lines
but who am I to tell you how to transcribe my ode
you gods have language   I don't I
only had a few words when I lived with you
and her
            With her, for twenty years
always at home   safe wherever she took me
was with me yes talking telling me things
beyond my brain
but not at all beyond my heart
she even taught me to gaze
into her eyes
never a habit of my kind   but one I learned
being, if I say so myself, very talented for a cat

IV
here's to you, a toast
a shot of Old Ghost

Reviewing the Tape

i.m. Piero Heliczer

I

calling 1959 calling 1959   what does he know
a red piano   a fragmentary tusk
he sees men & women preparing themselves
for the long journey across room

he is in love with the world
it's got a face like a horse
her hair is 365 poems   a tent   & into it
that tune   it's 1790! oops   he stops   goes back

sleeping is any handful earth
waking returns the toothbrush clack to the beaker
"her anger has caused me great pain"
can't tell which she he is talking about

brown photo   legend
man's reliance on fossil fuels but a short episode

II

no junipers no shouldn't think so no
he wrote   somewhere inside
so slow   a broken nose   repeating itself
into this hole in the ground

no connectives or interval music
it was hot in the dream hole
above the brick town with its captive dogs
the first time you saw it   acres of watery sand

ah to be funny in bed in writing

to be in our bodies
maybe it was just his old difficulty
of remaining in the upright position

of the higher primates
their glimmering moments of loving

III
the instruction manual lay soaking in the bilge
I'm yours I'm all yours   but the signals were garbled
one who looked tall rode away
didn't have much to say

narrative   pomp & pleasure
time in shore zones

ahead of the water they came
wrapped round a stick of incense
he'll sleep a long time
the day your son comes home

a flute & a spine in the grass
too dark   a raving madman
persistent cigarette burns on his hand & arm
november 1967   a hundred farmers plow to lucid murmurs

IV
to disappear   on the floor
in the other room   closing the book
"I'll be back in a minute"   flowers out there

over them reigned a red personage
in autumn some sponges   "i am moving
a fraction to the weaker taking"

218

this deep a breath is ardent
ultimate consummation of long ethereal affair
sit listening to the gods
approach her   their cries

it is peaceful peaceful
the people go crazy
the manager of this cinema
wears a big floppy heart ha ha

V
branching like any body
but here   have some wine
& exhale heaven   snug against her skin
kiss her   ill with love

"him now"   in his sleep he walks past it again
to one who lives there
in the rented satellite
with Officer No Quarter

enters another plane
of the new world   or drives the big white car
through savage people & frozen gases

still taping   his thoughts ran much upon this
wrote the works ever known as
the features of gods

VI
on the horse's back & into a hall
then son   simply expressing   in his own way
that I was wrong   6–9:00 A.M.
through customs in Hong Kong

all the way to her navel
a single large crystal
thinks of Don Giovanni
with no interference from tree-cutting crane

smileful girl   they used to spend maybe an hour
in glamorous roles
in a little while it won't exist

red mists of rage
plate glass breaks   snow streels in thoughts
across a green roof

VII
            "of Aegypt"

there is a light on   prudent alchemist
laughs like Leo the sun
crocodile curbs dangerous onslaught
Iaia of Kyzikos   her pagan will to realize

life in the sky   she saw
a tapir do the tango
prance from his mother's house
back where the night begins

in a seven-foot urn
I move about   the beetle wakes up
temporarily in charge of the 1920s

the surface extends all the way out to the core
wherever there is a hole distributed in space
cave equals room equals window

220

Survival Dancing

1995

For Ye Raven's Mistris
&
In Memoriam Sir Orfeo Joe

The title of this sequence was found on a laundromat bulletin board in upstate New York, in the early summer of 1994:

SURVIVAL DANCING
8 PM, Maplewood Park C.C.
May 12, 19, 26, June 2, 9
Call Bill 273-0126

Canto Arastra

opera creatures   technicolor elves
love to roam in profusion
make home in voices   shouting at no one
dotty shamans   pathos & farce transmitters
many birds singing waters gardens in Spain

    but time's grindstone jaws
    surely crunch graybeards
    & smoky lamplit ore
    in fatal history's central city
    sweep twenty years from day

    end of tube proclaims gone
    lineage guests broken drum virtuosi
    gone from free-bop survival dancing

now patriots of the dark
watch earth go silent movie

no poetry no pinball
no dream no pathos confusion
time was a placid pig
now is a shorter drift

    ride ice hold terror
    endure shadow
    light dim flares underground

faster than bubble life travels
metaphysicks away from the sun

    dark balance   every moment
    all gone   & going   things

In the Music Composed by Nutritious Algae

thought lined up pale winter
white sky
tall smooth car
loaded with motionless wings

staircase time
high speed nail into decades
curious shades of what happened
in small misunderstood group of being
engine loiters in thought

toss coin choose stairs a door with home
black hole of childhood
upholstered in cobblestones
mystery & exactitude of human nostrils

store babbling thought
see shadow body years ago
mumbling wooded mantra
gilded leisure morning

face down on tops of forest
begin to look at colors
they are air

then, mouth, what happens?
how did good very good happen?
question, indeed

Kindly Water Other Level

two found together   construct regard
place comb in hand   part knot exactly
look out windows   collect words

longing walk
bounces special

speak out strange
once daily

"she went right
clearing fence"

a few
still make sense

sing
awe
in joy's wise space

lie in bed
smell gigantic steamships
hug great-grandmother
wake up at dawn
well rested calm
afloat

a vivid weightless bean

Beginning & Ending with Lines from Christina Rossetti

strange voices sing among the planets
faint insect talk next door
cartoon mind   cartoon cantos
all the broken drums
La Châtelaine
hushes
her bandogs
& some of us speak weird(ly?)
(no; just weird)
but there is time
all around the time
we think is all the time
there is
your pleasure is my pleasure Earth
between walls of crickets
lips move in fluffed-up night
warm shrubs on slopes
dazzled heart thump rhododendron
grown old yet still so green

At This Point in L'Histoire

opaque air
                    ways to live
in a country of shadows
cold iron horse forests

done with hanging loose
jump out of sad speak
wrap bliss in tremulous pebbles

    "& how did the French
    revolution begin?"
    (vertical agitation)

laughs lakes willows lady
nests in dry wind on shore
book open
                    on mirror
"a nice walk with the dog"
 fast insect talk next door

Fair Poetry Eats Trembling Matter

Remote Omar
  lyrical bug
 or bearded time cloud
our public flits through earth
 belovéd yard of Allah

"Your century
   or mine?"
 My century
   My pleasure

"My dear that's dashing! Positively Valhallian!"
   — Christina *Plutarch?*
 or was it Ted for lunch with Rossetti . . .

all now remain in waters far from kin

 remains of enormous gringos
 punctuated by The Other

Was That Really a Sonnet?

"human being"
has government

    (thought
    you were so tiny

"real thoroughbred infinity"
this, we don't have in life

nevertheless &
thanks to you
I'm me once in a while

living this moment in English

"he tossed his clothes
into the past tense"

presence: really tough job
compared to natural flutter

Now On to Ghazal Gulch

"When did you last see your criteria?"
"Sometime . . . last winter . . . a minute ago . . ."

Pursue   the saying mind
please train of thought   throw samples

All breathe in some air
but someone needs to till the night

Shows him the miniature city: "Pity, really a pity
. . . possible hole in invention . . ."

Sorry I thought you person
I think I run into them

      (you look
      other, stroking
      her

Tiny figures
from the past
troop by
in pork pie hats

And why not
think of them as
"souls free of the body"

Gods Walked Animals Talked

trees in windy room
cicadas *possessed*

tall shadow weeds
    you page the heart
when was "think" first in sound?
walk through mind's middle
       human or rabbit
waves in tune with head

    eye coneflower
bright burning cells
    glad stomp & squeak
what progress after hawk?

megalith or mound
millions covered with snow
    or the great grease
of the longer than we
      (in living no TV)

best bet out of season
bones of gods
          posited universe
   wake up
smile in the giddy blue
join in the flash of was

    brains still on

The Word Thing

the brilliantly non-objective
appeared within
the century   (big introductory note
(a.k.a. Francis Ponge) many repeated preludes
                  & fun with angry young

century of the plunderbund
but book an object still recognized
words in tacit envelope
perpetuate
occasional whiff

trees suddenly active meme
in seasons' natural pedantry

method is effortless:
translation of autonomous objects
from adept to zygote
in rhapsodic rises & falls

next click, human language —
quite soon, physical density!
voice of things also includes
    steely twinkle in eye

ingenious it is
to have refined ear
ah, ancient ocher in graves

    aureous bodement, enigmagist fogbow
    century of the plunderbund
    nevertheless, satispassion
    tmesis   & terribilità

Si, Si, E.E.

warm legend, blue shadow:
"green day made gold tree"
light pulls love
in courtly poem
under other
tongue-sky, soul-grid, water, heart

years don't mark snow
nor skeletons' faces

sky train wind, nude moving so
words walk road
body, scene
(traverse child tiger light

but desert lives across targets
annuls cities
                    disquieted
leaves'
          memory: fire, war

muscle, take book, describe profile
thought follows
see for instance:
invisible nothing

eye forge battle blade

                              fall, shadow
                              ashes, fall

(& yes, they wore great big hats, size extra large

As Leaves Sweep Past

sister & Joe & Mistah Rilke
gone on "home"
                    small remote fish
on yesterday's pile of ashes

now, more people berserk
difficult demons, shattered dogs

no relief
            from this irony circus
end of tube essayistic
art a dead snakeskin
stuffed with live ants
        (& they return from your past
        grins on their silly mugs

eye meets moment, frame turns
sense looks to say what sense may say

        there, then, it hits:
        "you must change
        your terrible habits"

mocking gaze haunts myth
lyrical bug looks inside
happy to see old cloud
way up in the flying dust

& Time Trots By

sad glad hairy drives
top notch roaring suspense
oh the shaggy years

    hero food horny young sentences
    hot hero food pronto
    pronto   tilted charm never scratchy

(mad hatter at the bar
sometimes a ranting satan
rebuffed by furious foot)

    life does it
    think of it
    enjoy a think of it
    among the consequences

drive down Countdown Street
summer sad rearranged
by each day's killing power

beauty death power fear
remember
reside in sky with ears

    art
    loves
    funny details

    therefore is
    a dreaming
    & yes   joy!

    elitist   for sure

At Evenfall

recall enormous heave of moment
la vie en rose
before some Mallarméan blows it into the vide or abîme

   (but *timing egg in storm*
   beats driving car through rock
         — Albanian proverb

sun shadow fields cast loose
drum vibes in ground moths flutter
"O Lady Time, summer was great"

but now no house of letters stands
Elizabethanly enjoying given song
paradox knots each graduate

yet she'll stay up to read & write long letters
& on still tree-lined streets attend her musings
do art   eat well   never please wicked money

   always treat language like a dangerous toy

AHOE

And How on Earth

1997

"Robin Blaser once said in talking about a serial poem that it's as if you go into a room, a dark room, the light is turned on for a minute, then it's turned off again, and then you go into a different room where a light is turned on and turned off."

— Jack Spicer, from the Vancouver Lectures

"One could also see the face of another large apartment building there, whose windows at night would lighten or go dark in almost a curious narrative. I would imagine, sitting looking out, lives back of those windows, happy, sad, threatened, successful, always a little obscured and changing."

— Robert Creeley, *Coming Home*

"carve water, caress fire"

for Jane

Turn Off the News

anxiety gallops through chatter
fading century's martial insanities
brain struggles to sum up   "shut up"
articulation fails
walking shadow slides across faces

dusk over epitaphs
ash hair rusty litanies

dead friends and rain
paradise is an idiot

bones vines cold day

old vulture in airlock

scorpion dust
sneeze

O Ponder Bone of Fabled Carp

distant in time now,
maman
      equals pigeon

      duchess of echoes

      in hidden ruins'
      barefoot patter

memory seizes bundle, rides
horse of no illusion

ear tracks cricket blessings
clouds & echoes

translates, fabulates
umbrella afternoons

      arrow flashes
      the diminutive trembles

      in entourage of antennae
      gods hammer ears
      warlords groan exhausted

caress hair,
        lament tangle
in pale fits of ink

And Then There Are These
Skaldic Throwbacks . . .

wild Mara mind
    and wicked worm intensity
berserker travel on hushed sands
    longing for opiates of rain
        hawk's angle blue in bateau mist

battlement games
                grand gears of destiny

pikes under banner
                wild things pleading
thronged misery refined   laconic bards'

ear tackles era's phrasings in ironic runes

Head Sky Convoy Pattern

i.m. Franco Beltrametti

spirit murmur echoes
no letters from the dead

could this be winter
in the fifteenth century?

    (in mad orey-eyed paradiso
    inner brawler   favorite saber
    & that old piece of iron
    made to spew lead & belch smoke

Davy Crockett among astronauts
points out Earth is far

scholar of cheekbones & urbiculture
glows   hand him his favorite subject
shake out head

red windows   signs between perfect shapes
trees' feet still
glance moves over unknown waves

dreams chase moon
by suitcase steam wharf
face hair head equals passerby
masks float   speak

cloud stairs roof
house folds hums

words' wind   evening   cold birds scatter

    tone wall   flag rain   ear beam

      leaf tip holds dawn's door

Benign Evening Comedown

untwist antennae
shake out screen
blip on windows
dwell
on this wandering spoke

    in long instant of water murmur
    around us
    anthropoids
    small
    pleased
    and pleased to feel small and pleased

but that's too far back
this is not the sea
just a big puddle of hopeless desire
for a new brain
            for the species

Metaphor Mutaphor

sublunar fish philosophy
in temple pond

far from beaks of ignorance
heads quiet

night softer weave
no more tavern pain

rebel days' bright gallop over
no more perfect knowledge glyphs

but whose system happened?
shuttered minds' dark hole —

raise flag against sad experts
shout *we need windows!* this is an order!

into empty page / hard to read / desert wind

Hey, Dr. Who, Let's Dial 1965

in petaled decade glassy sunlight
tottering bliss in funhouse mirror pills
paludal billowing
                              in pad pavilions
delicate milk
wrote dwarf dream movies:

"Petrarch's Manhattan"
                              "The Wonders of You"

bodies, faces, chansons of surprise
bits of soft dust
                              soar in sombreros
into befuddled eyebrow thunderclouds
deep breaths make cages quiver
inspired milliseconds
                              tangled raga dark

and what else dreams the rain
                              dancers receding?

Leaves of Blur

aloft in eyes
quiet electric surprises
               (note rush —
old story soundtrack in mind's ear

danced down to the ships to sail
far past sun's orange mane
but we know what became of all that

cling to laconic chirps
weeds across face   glow gulp and write

rain on, past hearts   proud prowl in head
breathe mist on deep lens down the years

seen 'em come seen 'em go
a face or avenue   across blank page

        (said
         and
         undone

Script Mist

hang on to moment, naked, fair
frail as a butterfly — and where
did that come from?
from here, from under the leaves
of 1) lyrical moan, 2) sonorous foam

then the voice said "up and at them, hedgehog"
then it sat on his cool
with dark quark wings
while favorite sirens / mighty old voices
sang fierce and refined epitaphs

scattered and dashing, one does la-la more
at the good times institute
a joint in time
in the great carpentry

An Olive for Satie

easily whelmed by the past
long tangled thinker
traverses lake of mistake
revisiting sighs
& nothing's simplified
but out of that a touch
of animate grace
in thought's audible habitation
to point out earth, high liebesraum
& the way to fool's hill
to presence of world in her face

The Opening of the File

blue light
        chandelier blink! delight

pull rock from heavy head

  "ash tree bends to dawn"

page not "blank" but "fresh"

    door at noon

no longer bundle of distress
on slippery field of misfortune

but jovial irony machine
simultaneist presenter
    of elliptoid English:

    vibrant work, sage gestalt

ready to bless even depraved progenitors
to be a text to feel outrageous free
    intent on nonsense

      over here the plug
      to another figure there
      astride the request

ah, life in the fictive

hotly used
      in sensation's embrace

Emptier Planet

i.m. Larry Eigner

       a face

flies away

       while band plays on

a shake of beauty

         almost anyhow

     once more however

          gone

Jungle Finn

hommage à Schwitters

Enemy miss! And hiss, too! Tea yen, à la "See ya." Olé!
Inveigh! Then see Sally. Zen Celt? Aye, semper. Kate, in
yon car, maté-lickin' men! Ashbery, Hettie, mine tse-tse
coo, ten Voznesenskys. Wry Tio, vow. Noon za-zen, latte,
and a cough. Veal in oven, piss on tea; main rue, no den.
Neck key, Ma, gone. Mm, yass: am a peon. "Coo car, sah?"
Evokes Thai. Miss it. Yak-San ate Seurat. Ah. Intercon-
tinental Inn Pen sassed? Oh yeah. Tie tacks in Miz Cook's
ass. Zen, Homer, and linden. In ark is toe mess, yucks and
car doo. La. On Do Di nit. Hola! Ow, key rue non-code
Alta. Yon car Ité sue, then. Ashbery Thai Yevtushenko.
Hettie, mine tse-tse sees bat! Lola: Wax Pa's doxy. Scene at
ten, see bat, Manya wrecks it! Quaalude boo-hoo. Heave at
Yahweh scene, olé! Toot, Kim! He Zen. Ernie, ark is doity.
Hang in, Tilla, oh my coon, tea, hen, ass, tea. A. Vat. Eh? Sí.
Net Pooh, ooh, net "I." Yatter ate heel. I soothe old lute.

E. Quist

Time Rocking On

fell far from tribe
eagerly bloomed into drift

to wilt
at end of radical dream

ah utopia
          ah catastrophe
wild duck in eyes

(meant to say
"wild dusk in eyes"

but duck's okay
Ibsen, all that)

end of empire
weird with tears

no human head
          on this body politic
yet tree-born dignity
             inheres in a few
pray for quick magic
          a new verbarium

pass shell of sigh
          & raise to ear

Sur la terrasse

night train horn
reminder of nameless existence
brief insertions
bright and dark

o undulating gods
in night's open ark
courses of water and war
world's floaty news
an order has crashed
Petrarch in tundra
corpses wrapped in fog

what if long-practiced lyric
prove a dud
all wan and pale

before the unnameable
innumerable
now grazing earth
hoping for timely space ship

poetry this no-thing
drops into notebook air

in sea of air faint voices lift:
"eternity for little me"
dream forest felled at dawn
windless moon

go listen to some Locatelli
adrift in hist'rys drunken boat

Temple Noir

Images distributed about her, unceasingly, like moths: total-ized in cognitive map of hair specific to these exercises on the Trail of Death and Ruin, as preface to "adventure moment."

Notice she appeared gowned in actuality, and yet, as the other functions which followed her head leaped into instant anteriority, the dance became problematic.

There was much more to the same effect: precise lugubri-ousness.

The analytic craze was at its height, shriveling souls with sardonic laconicism in the foyer of instant fame — *her name:* it jerked up with murmured absentation — a coincidence she thought to emphasize, when her eye chanced to imagine this *referentiality* gazing at her, so *dialectical . . .*

Sails of Murmur

rose blade runs through beam
"face your water   cross no wiser"
long bones belch at chortling gators

remember motor hum   barouche in air
raise up favored rooms of past
erotic morphs
to animate thought's tactile habitation
opiates   echoes   hand them ashore

clarity hardly revisited
species a sneeze in eternity

unnerved by glyph lore
twinge   ride a slow gloom

but in a mouth be pleased
eager for the quiver
if it please the dawn

The Next Fifty Years

turn, tremble at honk
in dazed civil silence

wrong end? wrong beginning?
pain worms in

violent gloomy longings
of porky Agamemnons
in camouflage suits

city stilled   impossible pass

    "lay in *more,*
     master gold grub!"

work as owls, up here
stretch bridge
to where road starts again

Cat-Gods' Channel

we elegant erasers of mice

shall magick into pyramids

these sub-

urbs

you worked

like dogs

to build

inside the mind
she climbs
dazzling as apples, as thought

and so, with ancient yelps, we torch your maps

After the Newscast

past tribal heart's rusty twists
litanies of dagger, ropetree laments

sink or sail into mist
on bluer beam

quiver past
that past

to where the sleepers chirp
echoes of older wiser noise

of city deep in imagination's crystal
intelligence yearns for

    so come on up
    democracy
    it's time

Halo Blade

simple, it said   be mouth
   and will a piece of speak

(gods' voices belch and fold)

"thinker of sails, come up again"
tone wall moves on ear beam

you whirl in cylinder of rooms and days
sigh for a place beyond walls

   would it open your piano?
the past strikes many with nothing

they shiver   whelmed by purgatories
pile up habitations, dwell in sprawl

but the words bang your face
into the worlds   soon air and lights arrive

in fits of favorite city
revisited   turning
on to hum impossible dissident idiot love
in walking company
past winding sheets of thought
past violent echoes   hearts drift wiser
   into long tinge remembered

Silent Salad

retune ear
to curiosity
no fear of meaning's underside

remain
allochtonous
in pellucid hauteur

embrace memory
encode mnemonics
in forthcoming volumes:

> *Favonian Life*
> *American Jesus*
> *Toonlight Apocrypha*
> and
> *Atlantic Geheimnis*

> tell meaning to vanish
> & pray

Secret Cohesive Tactics

Blip off dim sunset. Blip on wild din sunrise!
Rise, Sun! Roar! Screen falls off
Falls off complicated
Fits of unreadable gridlock. Come sane, please?
Slow-lit mind skips out to prance,
Gods' summer legs delight green fool.
Love mind, mouse, moon,
& chansons, & cricket chirps.
Chase feast, unwind, let mind ships hover.
Hover, pencil shadow. First snooze, best snooze?
O dark ancestral snooze: spin yarn, hitch smoke —
Flower strange ways. Rise, sun, roar
On serendipitous dill brine,
Gather voice from house now ash and air.

Voice over Past House

rampant apprehension gone

sneeze twist remember trouble

wise old dog   tulips in bed

red green murmur turn-on

exactly walk

every stalk

come down slowly

write it back long thread

wing down corner zoom through stem

back to moon   or worm song

Caught with a Pronoun

"I have been quite content,
living on the poets' reservation"
— Friederike Mayröcker

the nanosecond before choice itself (?) occurs
check spell   uncoil from sheets
having a saying & even meaning
& no body without another

wrapped in deep skin
tangerine notes
that twitter up into mind's air
who for gods' sakes needs a "citational matrix"

let them remain
nailed down by their self-promotion
& me stay here   within the "confines of my agenda"

theory does look gray this morning
corporate colonization of human imagination
not allowed   on this reservation

Things to Do with Life

hang out with quantum generation
watch their terrible elegant dance

apply for job: editor of the universe
write: abrupt paint essential
write: glyph dog curiosity

ask: intergalactic thinking junked?
ask: democracy a blip on the screen?

stay at Hotel Nouvelle France
23 rue des Messageries
with ye raven's mistris

say there, there, surely not a time
for angel wings to be so public
pulse in mountain rhythm
"melancholy, unanswerable"

compose complicated fits
maintain ancient intimate anarch
stare at darkening trees on ridge
observe steadfast lights
look to save day into dark
   words write long laughter

out of once far ago
young splashings in snow
or old now in cherished chateau
where opal lightwave swoops
from l'oeil de ma Jeanne

Vibrant Ions

minutes
       selves
            socks

all one dune

          come again?

        I will

desire floats
      in a cyclone of dizzy cares

The Job

hushed, turned away
from uninspired diatribe platform

certain of being thoughts
alone but tactile

see bodies distilled in tragic nod
hear call: "wake, wizard!
cut time!
dispel this razor air, cold stratagems
    and whale anxiety"

in wild incessant years
                    dusk horses throng

air roars through aeons of babble
whispers laconic protocols

      prance advance to glimpse
      sprawl in realm of caw

smile on, not quite animate
in glorious timing of blue
and mostly excessive flit

Wings over Maximus

51 Pegasus a sun
has a planet
half the mass of Jupiter
too close to that sun
to have our kind of life

    looks at cigarette burn on mouse pad:
    "oh that'll just become familiar"

order in the saloon!

    helmeted angel waitresses
    out of 1890s Norwegian kitsch

      tilted loony toon light

    she used to laugh at his jokes
    but now he stands there in the cold & dark
    howling
    at her window
          (The Jilted Professor's Lament)

if feeling the absence
equals missing the presence

does missing the absence
equal feeling the presence?

    wild surmise
    in mild sunrise

      "& her name was Solitaire"

Hop through Intersection

collage dream of arms and the woman
and then through the and comes the *and*
a translation continuous
of moment's magnetic jaws
in country run on the principle
that you fool most of the people most of the time

fill in the stay-alive blanks
of dense wall chart experience

    let sonic awkwardness
    punch breath-holes in thought

write the plural   undermine the panopticon

      as one of the ear

An Or

wild empty leaps?
no, tango breakfast
in autoironic turban

daylight's allegoric air
impenetrable optics
insect creak or blink

rat muddy form
will drink
nocturnal rain decanter

adieu adieu Lili Marlene
(shush please)
or hum a dewy jinx

(or one comma there)

Apocrypha Hipponactea

fly likes smell of shit

☞

sweet flesh hope creatures
loiter, does, in browse fest
where dank lads roam on sassy paws
. . .
charmed subject entire[ly?]

☞

sillily jot swill slur

☞

endure future   crouched in cellars

☞

"I got *mine*. But I ain't got enough!"

☞

toss possible musical peony
gentle apparatus
into sudden sea

☞

you must assume that this
has nothing to do with you

Il y a

there is self-beast in season
                                    bright dew on grass
there is upon it that it
                        the sweetness
of festively followed call
                            of one in flight
there is approaching along a pensive way
a she   seems from the other side   hidden
cultivated
                beset by thought

there is dead fish in water
quickly changing into society's givens

there is stood tried to look across invisible sea
(some work for dark)
                            again away from window
(diligent messengers)

269

And What's *Your* Derivational Profile?

"Whammo Ammo, the ammo of choice
  for professional revolutionaries"

no thanks I'm on my motley crusade
to reach cells' dwelling (montage universe)

to praise proud trance, not witless boom
but drift & flicker
                              home
     in on beam of noble sorrow's
     anchored overture as heaven sleeps

"come close back once you held me when"
"name no longer on mail box"

water dance, shadow wash, no next time
jump-cuts, the works, vowels of hidden shaking
song of silent movie captions / captains

pick up stems of identity
                                   some time next year

Rundfunk

i.m. Helmut Heissenbüttel 1921–1996

follow blue fern to this eve's hostelry
glance at long broken results of Der Kapitalismus
back ago in mind's ear ghosts imprecate
years more eyes wild ions ah those very devil's years
war's dark harbors inspired many a toad
but a good horse objects to dead fountain
survived arm left on battlefield by fifty years
walk radio lights evening window course Totentag
spy Demeter stoned glad purple thoughts
come up with light and word beams fifty years
at war against smugdom spot in heart for black flag
even though we grow pale into dark nothing
night's rollers turn with tender uneasy weight

Earful of River Wind

back ago far
elevator to gray room

exquisite invisible hat
on transatlantic nakedness

but no instant citadel prospect
so goodbyes in port of old cactus planet

(end of old muse hour)

now paw in air
                    people demand dream

that still glance gnaws years

how many years
does it take to shut up
to learn to shut up

bones under trees
                    in a wrinkled light

down the toilet with old insight stew

September Song

thank you old tree
survivor of long-ago orchard

what's left of you now
is a bushel of apples
pile of dying wood

eat the apples
let wood go back in the ground

sad firs prowl hillsides in night rain
give me pathetic fallacy or give me pun

later in dream grunt coffin dialect
complaints about "extreme ersatz" and "finite Reich"
quite off the meter   way below frogman horizon

next day it's sunny & eighty degrees again

Your Turn

Dewdrop ode   sweet licks
In jokey code   Eat air!
Lose track of nights & days   dear melody
Fly me to Méjico?   no no

No reruns   hands   hair   snow
That's all we have for you today   but to-
Morrow, grace!   Sweet rain
Oaks bees old shoes & watches

Frogs will green again!
Energy roil   waves rock
Bright naked sun haze music play
In this old Pothole City of a brain

Vapors will brim light up slow pensive look
Make neurons dance in World Muse Impulse Book

Red Cats Revisited

wind-up bug
                    'moderne' wail
out of decrepit shop planks
bullets for nails they slung their zeal
new airs: hey, vodka!
bend, man, roll! look, shoes!
even if ings like that um some way yes can't
make talk elegant pants off Hemingway, oh man
the hulk digs buenos articles
immortal suitcase huge, wet, good

and strong, tears, frilly creeds
all that grave poking, mister, shriek another
but real time hate reruns the sky
perhaps so must to catacomb ground floor

years go inside to lunch in bowl
earth weeps to waters whispers future
crumpled dead slow envelope hereunder
feet do perch on marble spout
sky honey-born black steel twigs growl
world bright in tramcar once love ever rushed afloat
see, Master Fu, grave millions step by subway knees
with sacks of air mail for her sky machine

splendid as globe eye vaults the stare
enter hermetic front face mouth
bones glow in toy room there's no door
swarm day to feather chatter take fat family a while
listen to world grief red hot burden
xylophone output hand foot eyelids beds
down woods dark shutters slip
up dawn go houses crows stalk soft
smack motors rain whips rocky eyes
echo in blood pale songs pits wait

all ever round again blue murder hammers
hard trails spurt dust birds shuffle bright
dragonfly stumbles over cloud
profile ancient
                    meet face embossed
tall sputnik midnight snow forgetmenots

      stare away bottles
      across whirling field
      rune posters flap

And a Note:

In 1962, Lawrence Ferlinghetti's City Lights Books published in their Pocket Poets Series a small (64 pages) volume of poems by three Russian poets, in "English versions by Anselm Hollo," titled *Red Cats*. The back cover stated that "The translator . . . is a young Finnish poet living in London," which was true to the extent that I was twenty-eight years old, born in Finland, and working for the British Broadcasting Corporation in their European services.

In 1961, Ferlinghetti and Allen Ginsberg, with whom I had exchanged letters, became interested in American media reports of the literary "thaw" in Soviet Russia, and Ferlinghetti wrote to ask what I knew about the poets involved in that phenomenon. After some research in the BBC's and the British Museum Library's foreign periodicals holdings, I contacted my mother, Iris Walden-Hollo, a native of Riga (when it was part of Czarist Russia) and a fluent Russian speaker, and we collaborated on translations via the German (my first language; my own studies of Russian had never advanced beyond the alphabet).

After checking Mom's German 'literals' against some other translations into Swedish, Finnish, and German, I sent Ferlinghetti twenty-five poems by Yevgeni Yevtushenko, Andrei Voznesensky, and Semyon Kirsanov in English versions attempting to approximate what I then thought was 'hip' American English (Gilbert Sorrentino and Ted Berrigan later pointed out a number of embarrassing slips in

276

that diction). Ginsberg came up with the title, *Red Cats,* and, well, there it was, with a nice red and white brushwork cover by Ferlinghetti.

Now long out of print (my present copy is the sixth printing of 1968), it has been an amusing if at times irritating albatross: persons who have never read a line of my own work, or any of my later translations from languages I can truthfully say I'm familiar with (Paul Klee and Bertolt Brecht from the German, Paavo Haavikko and Pentti Saarikoski from the Finnish, Gunnar Harding and Olof Lagercrantz from the Swedish, Jean Genet's *Querelle* from the French, etc.), have spoken or written to me about the *Cats* with a nostalgic enthusiasm I find hard to share. With the possible exception of Voznesensky's *The Big Fire at the Architectural College,* the poems now strike me as simplistic, sentimental, and not a little hypocritical in their post- and sub-Mayakovskian rhetoric. It is also quite obvious that neither I nor any of their subsequent translators have been able to match whatever purely aural pleasures the originals may offer.

Thus the present text, "Red Cats Revisited," may perform a kind of personal exorcism; by chance methods and subsequent editorial intervention, all of its vocabulary (but not a single line or part of a line) was derived from the contents of the Pocket Poets book.

Hang on to Your Spell

restlessly wander alight on dwell in
big puddle oasis stay to magnify leaves
hang on to grief spoon listen
fair voices racked with patient stratagems
plots late afternoon questions old songs
bittersweet numbskull apocrypha
erotic morphs gowns rustling down blue tiles et cetera
entrancing farce in realm of hyperirony
aye forward script keep rolling them forever
red sails & vessels sway unhinged
for same old kumrad ready for the bell
even as gods grow pale
stone birds fall kerplunk from the air

After "Irish" by Paul Celan

"Mein Irisch Kind,
Wo weilest du?"

grant me
       wayleave

   up the granary ladder
to your sommeil

wayleave
       down the Somnus Trail

leave
   to cut peat
         on Heart's Incline
in the morn

Scripts

species began by accident
spread rose off plate
to make all other life hard
if not impossible
— Erna Melly

"5,351 writers of poems listed." Just one great big monologue project? Having one's saying, and even meaning. Love is a beast. The gift to be simple. Only it ain't so simple. Vanish, immediate body. Meld into dreams.

Similes out of simile bottle? Gaze verse? Gauze verse? WATCH OUT! *METAPHOR* OVERHEAD! INCOMING SIMILES!

Mild wind. Wild mind. O servants of sorrow, pray to St. Expedite when *fierce creatures* music gets too loud. Dark station. Mute rain. Taught how to be nothing but remembered face.

JOE had Grandpa Orph
grow happily old & gray
with Grandma Eurydice

HOMER his guy sail away
to the Apocryphal Isles

HOMER: (*nods*)

JOE: (*smiles, gently flaps his wings*)

⌒

Weave
     on rickety ladders
               between page & brain

       once in a while leap off

     do whirling dervish number

      then you-eff-oh it into starry noche

        "My script or yours?"

Good Radio
              & Good Night

Air

for J

"The air, that weightless something
that surrounds your head
and brightens when you laugh"
— Tonino Guerra

exiles from parallel worlds
we work our arts in this one
carve water, caress fire

the days run faster & faster
winter worms south then north again
now & again anxiety gallops through
wow who am you? are I? here, here

see presence of world in your face
clouds crickets weaving lights & glorious ache
that we be just as mortal as Signorina
Portinari whom Signor Alighieri once saw
(well, twice — so luckier we, for sure)

& as night falls, house folds around us, hums
faint flutes & tambourines
leave us asway in dreams in world's best bed

Sunset Caboose

"freight train, freight train
 going so fast"

old lights depart

brain's, heart's
gregarious troubles
take them out

one by one
to the great compost

but look at the bee
                        on its way
to what is brought out of light

AHOE 2

Johnny Cash Writes a Letter
to Santa Claus

1998

Arnaut Daniel
(a voice from the past):
" . . . who gathers the wind
who hunts with an ox
to chase a hare
forever, and swims against the current."

Jane:
At least half the time —

Anselm:
And so it was
and is
and this
another little boke
for you.

Passing Vapors

thought hands you strange balloons
Bon giorno! Presto! you're a farmer
you stumble over a cabbage
but mind bends cliffs   time slides
cleaves hearts   now you are grizzled old earl
playing flute in desert before the Saracens get you
the tune the one about freckled maidens
on the banks of the river Yarn   as the curved blade
takes your head off that morning
the color of quinces   the novel
slides from hand to floor
for fifteen seconds you dream of bombs and cabbage soup
then wake with a start to see any earlier "you"
now purely anecdotal subject

Big Furry Buddha in Back Yard

it's a made-up name
his real name is Bailey
all names are made-up

full moon &
our bats are back
bat is flutterer   fluttermouse

verbal tea leaves   interim moments
loony toon galaxy   at bottom of page cup

world symphony much the same
they've just added more instruments
place used to be run by two big bunches of liars
now there is only one big bunch

who cares   full moon &
our bats are back
bat is flutterer   fluttermouse

Lost Original

Mr. K. said   in times of great crudity
it is necessary   to be subtle
so please wrap around me
with awkward grace
I may have suffered some Rilke Damage
or do I just have a little trouble
with fantasy tripwires
while engrossed in the sky's lexicon
& hills like purple pachyderms
"there's been a great *upsurgence*"
said the announcer   but I didn't catch
what of   & what of where
does it come from where does it go
still asking   on down the road

Still Here & Here Again Then Here & Still

galactic dazzle dream talk & festina lente
high bounce transit moon gleam ambient creatures
inside has come outside inviting eye to read
the now   & then, the now
three seconds at a time
edges of moment gleam & turn
where are we now and now where are we now
this place alive with love & skill & care
the feast not movable but ever on the move
flaring & flashing through the wave barrage

Paint the Vacant Millennia

thought map   sea of paper   details of record
power fog   endless   above

minute written words
                            dusk pushes window
fate principle consoles (con-soles?)

slender moments   distant abysses
(never thought to use *that* word before)
evaporate backdrop charm

night strides along   endless objects approach
philosophy outside   dark trembling hull
loneliness presence your face branches
(anxiety of dim golden trance)

countless human drift   see twigs turn green
read what cannot be read   great animal faces

Much of It Unconscious Work but Work
(Said Francis Ponge)

pale afterglow on ridge
trees stand above
coal's underfoot pronouncements
same old quiet roar

dreamt younger or as now she may
see image fade to readability

or more like mice asleep for decades
    in time's backdrop corridors

brain twitters

bowstring slaps into wristguard

Hanging with Harpocrates

walk into dark verbarium   hit the switch

of course it's a drug   (addictive)
but you can't test it on rats

dreamchild bounds away
fades to well-behaved courage

take edge off lost music   face
Time's Godzilla Battalions

     step up, handsome thought

but all the days
you hoped would never come   will come

(your bandaged "pirate" mini-teddybear:
what was his name?)

      past composed recomposed

        a body runs past

Leave It to the Bonobos

Barrel out of Morpheus City's elliptical traffic, torrid, oneiric, pumped through raven's heart.

Unwind from sheet of exorbitant kisses, now back awake in world of Fourteenth Amendment: corporations as "persons" — thanks, Roscoe Conkling.

Golems, are they? They are, and they lord it over that world, determined to win the struggle with its desdichados (some of the latter now no longer wrapped in Red Flag but in the ectoplasms of Christ or Mahomet) (or cowering in the crannies of Theory Land — the Circle of Sciolists).

"Quelle époque!"

In gray dust angst, no shoal grace city. Or is it all just moving pictures in a box?

Crystallized Internet

being mystical I was gods
was a visual stuffed
deus ex melodrama
cold as a maiden from hell
mind out of subplot

"Kevin Kline reading Nietzsche in bed
 with large automatic weapon"

gibberish
with a few sharp thoughts thrown in
how lovely you are

related frequencies at work
in rattlesnake

colloquially brutal jouissance
of unfettered person

hovering on bushy wings
waiting for goodwill orchestra monoplane

    nonstop sensory triumph
    lit and shot
    in high duality

Sorrow Horse Music

creaky human continuum
seduced by daily lot
after remains of the day
(no encounters of the close kind)
on to headlights windings revelations
& things heard naked la nuit
veiled nestings   coils feed to antennae
all events occur in different places
& at different times while the i

    drop me in a glass
    where leaf or mouse is a message
    of silent evaporation
    forget lucky adjustments
    rain high above

    ("poetry in translation"
    — way too easy)

escapes its obligations into this writing
psyches itself to sound right
personal ways of eternal become line
literally filled with thinking

Old Cat Somber Moon

Running into feeling befuddles. A kiss, a moment, spiky, euphoric — then back to evolution. "It are the face on top." And this be nothing but croaks. Wintry mood floats in reason's mineshaft. First shapes, twilight trees, now they are doors. Then fades the sky around one. Looks like a heightened puddle, haloed by symbolic purples, "Cerebral, constructive, American worker will rise!" There was a time one would have ended this with "You don't say?" But that time's over. So let's hear it again: "Cerebral, constructive, American worker will rise!" O, K. All Right. Old cat howls, deaf now, at sixteen years, does not know where we are.

Presente or Not

watch stage constantly

      "honeycomb
                of floating thought"

   or just idle prattle
merely panoptic passions

fictional disquiet
               in decades of display
   which past   which present
never document

just secret stuff
you casual somnambule butterfly you
infinite text
          no wave jolt kisses
politics in a vase

need coat of alert forms
glimmer intensity of la muerte
writing at small depot of once-again
mind shooting filaments at subject

some small hell & what's it for
posthumous truffles
voice foretold but never close enough
for manifest dream fume

see the words opening
            their little beaks
dilemma ardent organic

   ever the window
   ever idle summer's
   secret fleurs

Philosophique

what
piped up
song
again

enjoys its
other

☞

"feel my book"
"format assistance received"

☞

thought maybe that was her
so drove round the block
but as I passed her again
she'd aged forty years

☞

lampshade
in the spider
night

☞

o handsome primates
of the past
your sudden doings

So Fix That Broken Axle

Then is it past   screeches of the mighty
"blood actions" Old Bird said
pondering   revolted
let us insinuate another song
"Art is my wife & myself"
turn this music on
for identity?   slept all evening
monotonous rush and purr
summer hard with the dead
The Edge   surely lovely
cannot be   a bed
"I am a behind
that grows a mind"
was that a
german joke?
sad-sack protagonist   depressed recluse
of sporadic human encounters

    "may note down what he sees
    among the ruins, for he sees
    other things and more than
    others; he is after all dead
    in his own lifetime, and is
    the true survivor" (Kafka)

but one is not that one is floaty yet anchored
"balloon on a string"
ship that sails both oceans and air
elevator that rises
through the clouds
or keeps going down

but no again it is a much smaller but truer
universe

Titled

We call it "titled" (example of good title)
Then use universal program
Characters strung on story
"Unkind Phenomena: A Story"
A certain heft and "boing!"
Words work   to look intended
"It works for wood, and walks on fell"
How long is greatest line?
It sounded full of recent pace
So I think, frogs. So it's very there.
The lovely instances of a kid's 1906.
Hilarious defended his ego:
"I met her in the lobby of the Bukowski Building."
To dream a letter   younger

The Ghostly Screen in Back of Things

high romance out of erasure
and combination: people still really had biplanes
and it was very adventurous
for persons called Beryl to fly them
back when they also had persons called The Original
The Genius   & The Muse
if not kept in the dark
they fade   except in the Wax Museum
where it is pretty dark   you may visit them there
it may bring some adventure into your life
move it forward a couple of centuries
through billions of words as old
as what we jokingly call mankind
"singing in moonlight by microphone tree"
if we gave this another title it would read differently

Just Another Bit of Scenery

essence of indescribable intention
one tries to recall
"he studied her body through tears"
actual text does not measure up

then there was the other thought
& the one after the other
it was carried up into the critical sky
but what was the music

did speech give reference to the body
now's the time to light a cigarette
pop in and out   as anyone in their right mind
would   save the words

that might make some interesting sense
next to each other   ambivalent minutes numbered
then hand your best inner sibling
a microphone   "her ass feels hot"

this microphone is a sculpture
so that's one level   now the only thing left
for us to do is this totally childish thing

Say Tango

in the silence of his attic
windows fold into dark

hoarsely the fire whispers
eighteenth century words

the adventure novelist
goes to his encyclopedias
to see what plants used to grow there & so on

while through his head
runs the not entirely impossible phrase

"Arose, aroused, the Duke of Ravensbruck..."

    but now for a sudden
    something-entirely-different tumble
    into say tango

or some quivery merde like that

now Daisy Aldan wouldn't have liked that
she would not have liked that at all

she just wanted M. Le Merveilleux
to settle in nicely for his bedtime read

A Hundred Mule Deer in the Back Yard

i.m. Allen Ginsberg

sleepwalkers' chess   condensare ad absurdum
why did we say what we just seem to have said
not a thought in our heads
is the thought in my head
meaning
meaning
          is a product
frame form work the old farm
stalking about like some mad Highlander
yet gigglily prudent as a bat's bellybutton
peering at words   "as if all worlds were there"
then think freedom music
not deplorable platforms
think lovely list of things   e.g.
Socialist Internationals Paris 1889 & Erfurt 1891:

> democracy & equal rights for all
>   including women
> separation of church & state
> free education
>   including higher education
> free medical service
> graduated taxes
> the eight-hour work day
> the right to organize unions

though serious revolvers
they stood no sporting chance

nor does the poet
walk around making hilarious remarks

don't shelve that book yet
I want to remember him a little longer

Ad Quodlibet

wheel around on best days   riding the hum
let coffee fumes spread across Dasein trail
& its perfect unconscious journals
avoid the wrongheaded
even when you can hear them
working up opinions
inside their unpleasant little brains
& the contemporary has aged
at least twenty years
& now has industrial presence of slag heap
just light a fire in the magic bag
spend evening by the well
raise cup of quest to speeding fugitive

We Are Having It Again and
Without Sorrow

molecular vessel named I Am December
gesticulates its way through mind maze
looking for some opaque you

    archy   old
& after reading les surréalistes some more

    now mental spin to winding woods
    in ancient jars brain slowly happened
    words come in spurts drool dream at dawn
    history from a tooth
    night grottoes of the blesséd matter
    in sleepwalk time no present face

rainy street no stars equals my language

now let us end
        with a discreet representation
   of a real lightbulb
still doing its connotations
      in a city of transparent sepulchers

off to ride
     last waltz railroad in November sun

Life in the Twists

bare freckled skin under black cloak
reminders of turns not taken or not taken well
endless parentheses faraway dogs
nighthawks crouched in basement cafeteria
with Rita Hayworth in her prime
more bitter than instant brewed
in aluminum pot on our way to the program
of was it social uplift or another 'summer of love'
between Dubuque and Sioux City

    "no let me tell you I am the phantom
    of the second life
    a wanderer a beautiful stray
    on the face of the earth"

    shook off the dust & put on her hat

      "all that was   ever is
      or vice versa . . ."

From the Notebooks of Professor Doppelganger

America still talk bizarre
falls off knocks versions about
stuff odd extensions
this has had bad maintaining

Eve's hand on Adam's inordinate elevation
individual lotus be that way
on day of Utopian items defined

news pinned on heart
as we wheel in to sleep's bright anagrams

she is the model in his dream life class
not having but having the seeing of her

these are our old forms

Give Me Big Shoes

In Western shoes   to die and go out in
's an easy religion
(as useful as dead
rat in refrigerator) so delete the messiah strain
but do not question prudent joy
SOMETIMES FIT   TO BURST WITH AMOR
think doting   think of Thinklife, Inc.:
"this version is the difficult *Sane*"

collective person enmeshed
in last bizarre Utopianism
human time spent maintaining
dictionaries on Platonic porch

response that looks like door
then becomes more intense

snow moon questions dwindle
pick up gaze from window
one among the shapes
begins to play

Hi, Haunting

back then it seemed he had more to say
than could be said in a lifetime
but there was time enough

year is a dome of sadness
"the big sleep"
"these stanzas are done"

the grand narratives are dead
the dead   are our grand narratives
the dreadful great

Skid Inside

any of every day
moment hung long
cut into cave

an all night parade
where you kiss people like pretty tarantulas
in the Oklahoma of the self

    Collision Alley
    bent defeat
    precisely your face

what if I glowed
closer to thee
mother of blaze & whippet food?

    in globe of night
    with puddles
    splash of quiet

coins   harbor   mystery   Ribcage Café
(obscure play: see illegible)

    out of the texts
    twilight exchanged
    in lopsided mouths' masquerade

Old Aristippus

night morn of glass
                         in cage of age
crystal pagination
adjust wild movement old heart
sleep by one present
                        as by a current

ah little oasis phrase:
"seated on his mobile trapeze
the aviator steers his ship
toward the four cardinal points"

then elevate activate leap into leaf
demand expression
                        demand window too

it's got to be true both ways
live and eat food before enormous general night

goodbye expensive time
                        say the murmurous measurers

Ultraista Oneiric

dream vortices broadcast
humorous din

from invisible ships of desire
in eddies of luminous sleep

     ¡Holá!

        bare feet in pitted mirror
      rarely unfolded planes
  in a blue shade

"where are the arms to go with these eyes?"
sumptuous figures in ample interiors

wave percussion over palpitating globe
swollen dynamos churn merchandise

naked silence   vast theater
    moonlit aerofoil memory
        bounces into unsteady calm

Attention: Selections Come on Tilted

do before reading approach yourself
emanate out as encouraging tale
speak a poem by everybody
stuff not craft   good long stuff
but then tons of blah
the almost whatever just folks
"what's wrong with these filters?"
chillier work stands up on new coasts
pivotal breaks   prior to pleasure
watch the thinking at times
back to a whereabouts
earlier perhaps wholesome denial
of no ideas   "Pluto is good"
then say you are just a line

The World as Fiasco

mais non Henri a dead man
can be a great traveling companion
mind's envelope sails
                              into destiny's breakfast
today was that day
I was going to be so busy
write cantos escape
crepuscular consumers'
                              revolving enclosures
on light speed sky trapeze
why *did* the chicken cross the road
Hemingway:
                    to die   in the rain
so good luck creating an atmosphere
where the honest cop
fears the crooked cop
said the 61-year-old former cop
in a ponytail
beard & earring who looked
more like an aging beat poet
which
            I'm not I'm not

Now O'clock

"Alone, this sudden darkness in a toybox."
— Ted Berrigan, Sonnet XXIX

mirror black for luck
click into motion our names
are we not paper?

glittering night talk stammered
strange sudden sad but not
old bulldog words drowned in shots
    of whiskey's seamless stairway
that was the wrong ticket that was

    some write "The Visions" but they can't write
    merely disturb the door
    to sudden darkness in toybox

when you return you return to poetry
a person said   this gave her poetry
measured considered worried
slow for some   minute music for others

    the former guard asleep now I did like it
    that them then   remember severely the era
    & its agreement gestures
    it's time it's life it's this like that
    what is a latch? what's wid dis paragraph?
    short tight rural news item   it ain't

wheels   low voices   syntax chant
tight sofa full of tinkling elements
proud semiology it snores

    among accessible presence traps
    some conscious mental quantum tropes of truth

shaped by timing   o tell it to come in

"Tempus? Fuggit!"

unbound from yonder level
       of oceans of presence
    yet crudely modeling such mutations
          just say on   just say off
    pace taken up by events
              population 'explained'
        that quantum clever too
    phenomena! refinement! thanks!
           modern words fail where how
    let the red bury their red
          or remarkable humorous hours as ever
    all day consider utopocalyptic
and then come breathing in and out
          to kiss confusion near the pond-
        erful joke about nonetheless
                scribble scrabble
but parked for breakfast thought continues
          to idle swoop and dazzle
        in loud formations over sound
                                   never dim

Johnny Cash Writes a Letter to Santa Claus

now too old to run away
(three months older than Donald Duck)
well they still seem to need me
& feed me at least some of them do
"Are you in the middle of something?"
"No I'm totally marginalized"
but still interested in these critters
walking lyrics to the grand abstruse song
     so singular they are
in their parts   assigned reassigned
& Lyn Hejinian quoted Shklovsky
"Role of Art — to kill Pessimism!"
translation not a matter of one to one
relationships any more than anything else is
Zophus the cat well pleased and even amazed
by his consciousness in successful leap

Notes

Poems age, just as people do. Some well, some not so well. This selection consists of parts of work written when I was in my early thirties, forties, fifties, and sixties, parts that have retained a modicum of resonance for me through all that time and up to the year 2000.

The title derives from Louis Zukofsky's "A Statement for Poetry" (1950): "No verse is 'free,' however, if its rhythms inevitably carry the words in contexts that do not falsify the function of words as speech probing *the possibilities and attractions of existence. This being the practice of poetry,* prosody as such is of secondary interest to the poet. He looks, so to speak, into his ear as he does at the same time into his heart and intellect." [italics mine]

☞ from THE COHERENCES

Introduction
True anecdote, or, as true as anecdotes are . . . César Vallejo (1892-1917); Peruvian; great Modernist of the Hispanophone world; died of starvation; in Paris.

Instances
From *The Odyssey* (mine and the original).

☞ from MAYA

In the Octagonal Room
This was the octagonal room in the ("old") Tate Gallery in London, for a long time devoted to works by William Blake and Samuel Palmer.

☞ from SENSATION 27

Sensation 27 derived its title from being Number 27 in a series called "a curriculum of the soul," published by John Clarke and Albert Glover of the Institute of Further Studies. The curriculum had been drafted by Charles Olson when he taught, briefly, at SUNY Buffalo; Clarke & Glover assigned "Sensation" to me.

At This point . . .
"while down below in Iowa City / a small Dane is freaking out in a drugstore" — the late lamented Pol Borum, distinguished poet, critic, translator of U.S. American poetry, who found the late U.S. sixties a little too heady, even in idyllic Iowa City. But he did survive them.

After Verlaine
Verlaine's famous lines are "it rains on the city / as it rains in my heart."

To Be Born Again
"th-there's a l-lot of" etc. — what the good doctor told an interlocutor, late in life.

☞ from FINITE CONTINUED

The Years
Not autobiographical. Every sentence in the text can be found in Mr. Bukowski's prose works.

☞ from NO COMPLAINTS

Songs of the Sentence Cubes
The "sentence cubes" were precursors of the more recent "Magnetic Poetry Kits."

Ten Cheremiss (Mari) Songs
These versions were based on Finnish translations made by Marjukka and Jorma Eronen, published in 1979. The Mari are a "Finnic" people.

☞ from NEAR MISS HAIKU

Les Américains
Notes from an extraordinarily complex bus ride from Boulder, Colorado, to Salt Lake City, Utah.

☞ from CORVUS

A Town Dedicated to the Pursuit of Fitness and Inner Peace
Title borrowed from a health-food magazine article on Boulder, Colorado, where the scribe resides.

Inhabited Eyes
"falcon-eyed Montcorbier" — François Villon (his 'real' name).

Why There Is a Cat Curfew in Our House
Procyon: Greek for "before the dog," name of a star near Orion that rises a little earlier than Sirius, the "Dog Star," and also the scientific name for the raccoon.

Blue Ceiling
"never admit you're rich or asleep" — "I have never known a man to admit that he was either rich or asleep" — Patrick O'Brian, *Master and Commander.* "what's

ragged should be left ragged" — Ludwig Wittgenstein, *Culture and Value.* "mad as Cassandra . . .": "the wind mad as Cassandra / who was as sane as the lot of 'em" — Ezra Pound, *The Cantos.* "the love that moves . . .": Dante.

Pterodactyls

I: "Publication date first of October": In the summer of 1993, I translated (from a fast and carefree French translation!) *War Journal* by Zlatko Dizdarevic, the then-editor of Sarajevo's only surviving newspaper *Oslobodjenje*. The English-language edition of the book was published by Fromm International, New York, in 1994. "convivencia": The period, 711-1492 C.E., in which Jews, Muslims, and Christians coexisted in the abundant civilization of al-Andalus in what is now Spain. "The art of being a slave is to rule one's master": Diogenes. IV: This was written in Salt Lake City, Utah (= Deseret, in LDS parlance), in the mid-eighties, thus quite some time before a certain self-styled Serb "poet" began a war of genocide and extermination against Bosnia and specifically its capital, Sarajevo. Tomaž Šalamun is the greatest living poet of dead Yugoslavia, and now, mercifully, still-alive Slovenia. "son, write longer lines": my father told me that, a thousand years ago.

☞ from SURVIVAL DANCING

Canto Arastra

"arastra": Millstone(s) used to grind up ore; probably from Spanish *arar*, to till. First noted both word and object on a drive to Central City, Colorado, an old mining town now abandoned to slot machines, with Joe Cardarelli in late April 1994. Four months later, Joe, a lovely poet, painter, and dear friend, suddenly departed from the human universe. *Survival Dancing* is dedicated to his memory.

Beginning & Ending with Lines from Christina Rossetti

"La Châtelaine": The mistress of a chateau. "her bandogs": Dogs kept tied to serve as watchdogs or because of their ferocity. The medievalism harks back to a dream Paul Blackburn once told me, and to my reading of William Watson's excellent novels *The Knight on the Bridge* and *Beltran in Exile*.

At This Point in L'Histoire

"& how did the French / revolution begin?": Alas, that day (in was it 1946?) I had not memorized the relevant page in my history textbook; all I was able to come up with, under the history teacher's stern gaze, was the first sentence of that descriptive prose: "On the fourteenth of July, all the church bells of Paris began to toll . . ."

Fair Poetry Eats Trembling Matter

"Remote Omar": Apart from its enjoyable interior resonance, the line refers to Persian poet Omar Khayyám (? — c. 1133) who was memorably Englished by

Edward Fitzgerald (1809-1883) and later quoted by Ogden Nash (1902-1971) in his lines "I myself am more and more inclined to agree with Omar and Satchel Paige (c. 1906-1982) as I grow older: / Don't try to rewrite what the moving finger has writ, and don't ever look over your shoulder." ". . . Positively Valhallian": Valhalla was the pleasure dome to which slain Scandinavian warriors were transported from the battlefield by large and fierce angelic females, known as Valkyries, for continuous after-hours entertainment until the end of the world (a.k.a. Ragnarök). " — Christina Plutarch?": Clearly, a brief moment of confusion on the intergalactic internet — possibly even a flashback from a future when Christina Rossetti (1830-1894) and Mestrius Plutarchus (c. 48-c. 121), both of them writers on philosophical subjects, may seem practically contemporary. A prolific educational author whose influence extended well into medieval times, Plutarch spent the last thirty years of his life as a priest at Delphi. Rossetti was a celibate priestess of the High Anglican deity, her last work being *The Face of the Deep: A Devotional Commentary on the Apocalypse*. "or was it Ted for lunch with Rossetti . . .": The Rossetti of this line could also be Christina's brother, Dante Gabriel (1828-82), poet, painter, and translator, whose turbulent career as a member of the Pre-Raphaelite Brotherhood would seem more compatible with the life and times of New York School member Ted Berrigan (1934-1983), poet of major verbal leaps and bounds both at, and even when out to, lunch. The scribe suspects, however, that it is Christina, to whose sonnets a younger critic has recently compared Ted's work (happily available again from Penguin). Unlike either Christina or Dante Gabriel, Ted liked to refer to friends in his poems by their first names. The scribe regrets any possible confusion arising out of his adoption of this practice; now that you know which Ted is intended, you should hasten to the nearest book emporium and acquire a copy of *The Sonnets*. It will restore *some* sanity to your life.

Commentary: The 'author', who is quite postmodernly used to dwelling inside inverted commas, and prefers the term 'scribe', is invoking a number of temporal precursors and considering the ways in which their "fair poetry" ("fair" in *any* sense) ingests their "trembling matter" and possibly survives for a while (until Ragnarök) in some noncorporeal form, while the corporeal ones are transmuted into "bug" or "cloud," and the "public" also "flits through earth." The play on "remain" and "remains" in the last three lines may, tangentially, refer to theoretical and canonical arguments of recent years.

Was That Really a Sonnet?

No names in this one, but three sets of full quotation marks. Most days, it can seem quite hard to utter the term "human being" with a straight face. As for whether it "has government," well, this country presently seems in the clutches of what Ezra Pound describes in Canto LXII (paraphrasing John Adams): "republican jealousy which seeks to cut off all power / from fear of abuses does / quite as much harm as a despotism." "real thoroughbred infinity" is an equally nice but questionable notion, and "he tossed his clothes / into the past tense" is a moment of old-time narrative that may indicate the futility of attempts to describe spontaneous abandon. The two *you*s in the text may be one and the same; the *I* claiming to be *me* "once in a while" probably is. The title is really an afterthought and may be spoken by the reader.

The Word Thing
"(a.k.a. Francis Ponge)": (1899-1988), author of *Le parti pris des choses* ("Taking the Side of Things") and many other books of poetic meditation on "word" and "thing." "century of the plunderbund": *Plunderbund* — a league of commercial, political, or financial interests that exploits the public. "trees suddenly active *meme*": A *meme* is to your culture as a gene is to your body. "aureous bodement, enigmagist fogbow": The "enigmagists" were a loosely knit group of young poets attending the Jack Kerouac School of Disembodied Poetics in 1994-5. "nevertheless, satispassion / tmesis & terribilità": *Satispassion* — penitential suffering; *tmesis* — the separation of the elements of a compound word by the interposition of another word or words, e.g. "far effin' out"; *terribilità* — effort or expression of powerful will and immense angry force.

Si, Si, E.E.
cummings, who else.

As Leaves Sweep Past
"art a dead snakeskin": Statement attributed to Ingmar Bergman by Swedish critic Leif Zern in his book *Se Bergman* ("See Bergman"), 1993. "you must change / your terrible habits": Paraphrase of Rilke's "You must change your life."

At Evenfall
"la vie en rose": French pop song the scribe remembers from his childhood, sung by Edith Piaf and the scribe's sister. ". . . blows it into the *vide* or *abime*": "void" and "abyss," two concepts / words much favored by French Modernist (and even postmodernist) poets, over American / English "empty" (or e-ness) and "hole." Rilke's poem "Autumn" is echoed in the lines "O Lady Time, summer was great," "stay up to read . . . " "still tree-lined streets." "always treat language like a dangerous toy": "Out of the green trees across snow as pure as salt. It is so pure it treats English like a toy." — Edward Dorn, Afterword to *Sojourner Microcosms*.

☞ from AHOE (And How on Earth)

Turn Off the News
"fading century's martial insanities": Possibly no worse than any other century's, except in a quantitative sense. But this is where thought tends to fracture.

O Ponder Bone of Fabled Carp
"maman equals pigeon": Brief epiphany in the plaza outside the Pompidou Center — the scribe realized how similar his (dear departed) mother's bearing and protective-aggressive behavior was to that of *pigeons.*

The once-upon-a-time modernity of the Pompidou may also have reminded him of certain "moderne" parts of Stockholm in the nineteen-forties, where *maman* once whacked him across the nose with her umbrella.

And Then There Are These Skaldic Throwbacks . . .
Eurasian "Middle" and "Dark" "Ages" still flash onto the screen with some frequency. Egil Skallagrimsson's life saga stands on the scribe's shelf, next to Watson's *The Knight on the Bridge* and Evan S. Connell's *Deus Lo Volt.* There is mucho machismo / in medievalismo, for sure, but there also are records of remarkable women, strong, gifted, and adorable. (It's still OK to say adorable, isn't it?)

Head Sky Convoy Pattern
Franco Beltrametti (1937-1995), Swiss-Italian truly cosmopolitan poet, painter, publisher, world traveler. I only met him once, in Salt Lake City of all places — he was "passing through" — but he was and remains a significant and encouraging constellation in my interior sky. "Davy Crockett among [the] astronauts": Ted Berrigan, another great constellation, called himself that in a lecture he gave at 80 Langton Street in San Francisco on June 24, 1981. The third, open-parenthesis, stanza marks a brief reappearance of the "skaldic throwback" rage that in the scribe's psyche always accompanies the news of friends' (always) untimely deaths.

Benign Evening Comedown
The middle stanza refers to Elaine Morgan's delightful book *The Descent of Woman,* read many years ago.

Metaphor Mutaphor
After its "Chinese" beginning, the poem moves on to consider la vida, and its passing, and once again, Utopia . . .

Hey, Dr. Who, Let's Dial 1965
You were there, too. Some of you.

Leaves of Blur
"old story soundtrack" fading "like" "mist on deep lens down the years." (Similes perhaps more permissible in footnotes?)

An Olive for Satie
Composer Erik Satie is said to have titled some of his shorter works according to whatever his gaze came to rest on after he had penned the last note. *Liebesraum:* approximately "love space" — a neologism echoing the lexically 'real' words *Liebestraum* ("dream of love") and *Lebensraum* ("life space" — another German word ruined by the Nazis, who used it to express their idea that their empire should encompass all of Europe, Asia, and Africa).

324

The Opening of the File
"jovial irony machine": May have been thinking of Marcel Duchamp. The title refers to both Robert Duncan's *The Opening of the Field* and the personal computer.

Jungle Finn
A homage to one of the fathers of "sound poetry," Kurt Schwitters, composed by homeophonic translation of a text Finnish poet and painter Jyrki Pellinen wrote on the occasion of John Ashbery's reading at the Helsinki Festival. No data available on E. Quist, the presumed author.

Sur la terrasse
"To build the city of Dioce whose terraces are the color of stars." EP, Canto LXXIV. "Ecbatana, ancient capital of Media Magna, founded in 6th century B.C.E by the legendary first king of the Medes, Deïoces. According to Herodotus, the city was surrounded by seven concentric walls, each a different color..." Edwards and Vasse, *Annotated Index to the Cantos of Ezra Pound,* (U of CA Press, 1957). "Petrarch in tundra" — thinking about Osip Mandelshtam. Locatelli — eighteenth-century composer discovered via Patrick O'Brian's monumental Aubrey / Maturin novels: his music is in the protagonists' (a sturdy sea captain and his ship's surgeon) repertoire.

Temple Noir
Written in the scribe's "Cut-Up: Before and After" class. Lives intersecting in the mind.

The Next Fifty Years
"stretch bridge": Too bad that this now echoes a cliché promoted by the Prez from Arkansaw.

Cat-Gods' Channel
What if cats, etc.? And who is "she [who] climbs"?

Halo Blade
"in fits of favorite city": The "New York of the Mind" (as in quite a few of these).

Silent Salad
Not sure those "forthcoming volumes" will be written in this dimension.

Wings over Maximus
Zoom shots — from cosmological ("Maximus"/ Olson) vistas to 'realtime' flyspecks, on to fantasy, anecdotal recollection of an aging academic's problems, Derrida on absence and presence, and a name from an Ian Fleming novel. Voilà!

Apocrypha Hipponactea
See *Hipponax of Ephesus,* translated by Anselm Hollo (Baltimore, Tropos Press, 1995). These fragments are "in the manner of."

Il y a
One impetus for this was the relative untranslatability of Guillaume Apollinaire's poem of the same title, due to the absence of an English locution as loose and comprehensive (at once) as the French "Il y a."

Rundfunk
One-armed like Blaise Cendrars (the left "left," as they say, on some dismal battlefield in 1942), tall, calm, funny, and erudite, German poet Helmut Heissenbüttel had (as he put it) "a lasting soft spot for the black banner of anarchy. My innermost conviction is anarcho-syndicalist. Never mind that I know it (anarcho-syndicalism) can never be realized, but that is where my secret love lies." Rosmarie Waldrop's and Pierre Joris's translations from his work are excellent: Heissenbüttel is far from 'easy,' somewhere between Clark Coolidge and *Finnegans Wake* on the translation meter.

After "Irish" by Paul Celan
Result of Alec Finlay's commission to attempt a translation of Celan's poem "Irisch." Epigraph ("My Irish child, / Where tarriest thou?") from Wagner's *Tristan und Isolde,* quoted by T.S. Eliot in lines 33-34 of *The Waste Land.* "Sleep" does not match the weight of "Schlaf" in Celan's poem; recourse was taken to French "sommeil" and Latin "somnus."

Scripts
Erna Melly, author of the epigraph, may be related both to Ern Malley, father figure of modern Australian poetry, and George Melly, the great British jazz and art critic and creator of the comic strip *Flook.* See *The Ern Malley Affair* by Michael Heyward (London, Faber & Faber, 1993). "JOE," here, is the poet Joe Cardarelli (1944-1994), author of *The Unknown Story of Orpheus (A Work Unfinished).*

Sunset Caboose
Ideally, the first two lines should be sung in the inimitably nasal voice of Nancy Whiskey (RCCD 3007, *Freight Train: The Chas McDevitt Skiffle Group*).

☞ from AHOE 2 (Johnny Cash Writes a Letter to Santa Claus)

Hanging with Harpocrates
Harpocrates — god of silence (hence, "Harpo" Marx).

Leave it to the Bonobos
"Bonobos" — primate cousins who "Make Love Not War." "Circle of Sciolists" — sciolism: "superficial show of learning." *"Quelle époque"* — "what an epoch (we live in)!"

Sorrow Horse Music
Epigraph: Utah Phillips is a wonderful American folk singer and storyteller still roaming the West.

Presente or Not "Glimmer intensity of la muerte": La muerte — Spanish six-letter word. Wonder why I didn't put it in italics (see note to *Say Tango*). "secret fleurs": French flowers.

So Fix that Broken Axle
"Old Bird": A 'character' in "West Is Left on the Map" *(Corvus,* Coffee House Press, 1995).

Titled
"'I met her in the lobby of . . .'": See *The Years: I.M. Charles Bukowski.*

The Ghostly Screen in Back of Things
"biplanes . . . persons called Beryl": Legend (quite possibly apocryphal) has it that John Ashbery composed his poem "Europe" (in *The Tennis Court Oath,* Wesleyan, 1962) by means of erasure out of a juvenile novel called *Beryl in Her Biplane.*

Just Another Bit of Scenery
"'her ass feels hot'": Translation of *L.H.O.O.Q.* (Duchamp's title for his mustachioed Mona Lisa).

Say Tango
"Arose, aroused . . .'": Inspired, no doubt, by a brief dip into the interminable text production of the late Barbara Cartland. "or some quivery merde . . .": French five-letter word. "now Daisy Aldan . . .": Noted New York editor, art critic, writer of poems, who complained in a review (in a publication hubristically titled *World Literature Today*) of my book *Outlying Districts* that it contained too many four-letter words and not enough of The Marvelous.

Ad Quodlibet
"disputatio ad quodlibet" (Latin): disputation on anything whatsoever. "Dasein" (German): "existence," literally "there-being."

We Are Having It Again and Without Sorrow
Title from Ernest Hemingway's *Across the River and into the Trees:* "We are having fun," the girl said. "We are having it again and without sorrow." "archy": Don Marquis's immortal protagonist in *Archy and Mehitabel.*

Give Me Big Shoes

Title from Nike TV commercial for hiking shoes, shot in Kenya using Samburu tribesmen. Camera closes in on tribesman who speaks his native language, Maa. As he speaks, the slogan "Just Do It" appears on the screen. Lee Cronk, anthropologist at the U of Cincinnati, says the man is really saying: "I don't want these. Give me big shoes." Says Nike's Elizabeth Dolan: "We thought nobody in America would know what he said."

Hi, Haunting

"the big sleep" — Raymond Chandler. "these stanzas are done" — Gertrude Stein.

Old Aristippus

Title refers to Aristippus (2), grandson of Socrates' eponymous companion, founder of the Cyrenaic school. "He appears to have been the first to teach . . . that immediate pleasure was the only end of action . . . the present moment is the only reality." *(Oxford Classical Dictionary,* 1992 edition) "seated on his mobile trapeze . . .": lines from a poem by poet Rafael Lasso de la Vega (1890-1959), one of the principal proponents of the Dada movement in Spain.

Ultraista Oneiric

Title: Spanish Dadas called themselves Ultraistas. Oneiric: pertaining to the realm of dreaming. *"¡Holá!":* What German tourists shout to indicate their approval at muy folklórico performances. muy folklórico: Very ethnic and / or kitschy; mostly kitschy.

The World as Fiasco

"mais non Henri": Henri Michaux, who warned against traveling with a dead man (see also Jim Jarmusch's film *Dead Man).* "61-year-old former cop": Serpico, testifying to New York City Council on police brutality and crooked cops on the twenty-third of September 1997.

"Tempus? Fuggit!"

"utopocalyptic": term coined by poet Michael Heller: "that odd socio-political or cultural product, both fever and exacerbation, in which an individual is torn between idealized hopes and gnawing dread."

Poetry Titles from Coffee House Press

The Green Lake Is Awake by Joseph Ceravolo
Easter Sunday by Tom Clark
87 North by Michael Coffey
Panoramas by Victor Hernández Cruz
Red Beans by Victor Hernández Cruz
Madame Deluxe by Tenaya Darlington
Routine Disruptions by Kenward Elmslie
Decoy by Elaine Equi
Surface Tension by Elaine Equi
Voice-Over by Elaine Equi
Shiny Pencils at the Edge of Things by Dick Gallup
The Book of Medicines by Linda Hogan
Savings by Linda Hogan
Corvus by Anselm Hollo
Outlying Districts by Anselm Hollo
Pick Up the House by Anselm Hollo
Drawing the Line by Lawson Fusao Inada
Legends from Camp by Lawson Fusao Inada
Teducation by Ted Joans
Cranial Guitar by Bob Kaufman
Cant Be Wrong by Michael Lally
Paul Metcalf: Collected Works, Volume I, 1956 – 1976
Paul Metcalf: Collected Works, Volume II, 1976 – 1986
Paul Metcalf: Collected Works, Volume III, 1987 – 1997
Margaret & Dusty by Alice Notley
Revenants by Mark Nowak
Great Balls of Fire by Ron Padgett
Of Flesh & Spirit by Wang Ping
Thirsting for Peace in a Raging Century by Edward Sanders
Earliest Worlds by Eleni Sikelianos
Clinch by Michael Scholnick
Avalanche by Quincy Troupe
Choruses by Quincy Troupe
Breakers by Paul Violi
Helping the Dreamer by Anne Waldman
Iovis: All Is Full of Jove by Anne Waldman
Iovis Book II by Anne Waldman
Nice to See You: Homage to Ted Berrigan Anne Waldman, editor
The Annotated "Here" by Marjorie Welish